Europeanizing Education:
governing a new policy space

Europeanizing Education:
governing a new policy space

MARTIN LAWN & SOTIRIA GREK

SYMPOSIUM
BOOKS

Symposium Books Ltd
PO Box 204, Didcot, Oxford OX11 9ZQ, United Kingdom
www.symposium-books.co.uk

Published in the United Kingdom, 2012

ISBN 978-1-873927-61-8

Printed and bound in the United Kingdom by Hobbs the Printers, Southampton
www.hobbs.uk.com

Contents

CHAPTER 1

Introduction

The study of common, diverse or even oppositional effects in the field of education across Europe today is a growing field of inquiry and research, as a result of many actions and programmes which have grown in volume and complexity in the last few decades, and the development of common European education policies. The construction of policy spaces by the European Union (EU) makes Europe governable but the means and acts of governing Europe appear to be particular to it and at times opaque; they are reflections of the problems of diverse national jurisdictions, new network organization, market solutions and politics. During the last few decades, education as a field has become multifaceted, and has been redefined as lifelong learning; as such, it occupies a central role in different fields of public policy and has become a way of mobilizing and governing the European space of education, a new policy space.

Studying Europeanizing effects across the field of education has become a necessary but complex task; in any case, this is not the way that the field of education forms and studies its problems. Thinking about education and its systems is still bordered by the limitations of nation-state histories, language and vernacular customs. Boundaries of thought are not just disciplinary or even customary; they are literally framed by spatial limits. Researching across political borders means exploring other ways of understanding education, embedded within landscapes comprised of histories of national policy documents, law and legislation, accumulated commentaries and normative engagements. Educational researchers produce habits of exclusion by which awkward knowledge, that is, knowledge drawn from across the border, is often isolated, pushed back or labelled exotic and irrelevant. Cross-border travellers are absentees; expert at crossing boundaries, their tales are excluded from an understanding of the bordered narrative of the research case. The commonality of concepts in education, often through a process of Anglicization, disguises the lack of consensus on their cultural meanings: the use of quality or accountability or 'learning', all key terms today, overlooks their lack of translation or univocal meaning across cultural contexts. Borders are crossed by new global or at least European members, bearing a new magic of words. New terms – knowledge society, quality assurance, knowledge economy, learning economy – while economizing the language of education and signalling important, new directions, have to bear the weight of local incomprehension.

At the same time, states and their economies change. The speed, scale and products of change imposed by trade and the 'market' upon the national systems of governing, and the place of the education system within them, is a contemporary issue for education research. The subject of study – the state, systems of education and the nation – appears to be becoming unstable and transitory. It is not easily contained by its 'natural' – that is, its 'constructed' – borders. Nation-states are becoming less important in the new world order, and so is their contained national education. Education is being transmitted and traded via different kinds of satellite, cable and Internet. Crossing borders might also mean losing control to global norms. The international and the global appear as explanatory terms in the most embedded national educational arenas to justify change, and as bearers of cross-borders meanings, language and text, they wrap policy, regulation and proposals. Crossing state borders is present in the bilateral arrangements in education in which states transfer, borrow or learn from other practices. This process of internationalization, in which political boundaries are suspended, has an equivalent in the global economic processes by which borders are dissolved. The subject of study is not able to easily manage the transformation of its subjects. Global and regional shifts in people, culture, food, information and transport have effects within borders on mentality, governing, and the ordering of education as a service and a way of thinking and researching. It is not so easy to retain borders around the subject and exclude awkward knowledge.

It is in this context that the study of Europeanizing processes in education takes place. The ideas of Europeanization that we are using to define our work contain several explanatory elements reflecting the complexity of processes which include, first, transnational flows and networks of people, ideas and practices across European borders; second, direct effects of EU policy; and, finally, the Europeanizing effect of international institutions and globalization. This approach is not the most common way of approaching the study of Europe, which tends to follow problems of political integration and aspects of multilevel governance. We are taking a wider view, focusing on the intended and unintended consequences of European processes, and the relational effects of disparate but powerful European agencies and actors. We see three key elements in these processes:

1. The invention of a new space of work, thinking and policy by network, associations and elites across Europe and the significance of national and European actors in constructing this space, through the flow of policy ideas, knowledge and data, and practices from place to

place, sector to sector, organization to organization, and across borders. Education work itself varies and is now tightly or loosely connected to the national context.

2. The direct creation of a shared policy space or spaces as a result of regulation or policy momentum in particular fields, and the overall governing of the EU, especially through the open method of coordination; the field of education, as a single, commensurable space has been increasingly configured and formed within this political context. Apart from the moral formal governing processes, education in Europe has also been largely steered through comparison and the rise of numerical data. Governing the complexity of Europe is now viewed as a problem of data and benchmarking.

3. The convolutions and intricacies of Europeanization processes are compounded by the continuing effects of globalization and the changing national, a constant cycle of influences which denies hierarchy or dominant actors, and is present in the public and the private spheres.

These three dimensions do not describe a homogeneous Europe but one which has common features: it is open to the market, it seeks to create a union which manages risk, and it governs itself by consensus and regulation. Europeanization is the process of formation of the European Union, the processes which are attached loosely or formally to this formation, or set in motion by it. Yet it is also a political, spatial, networked phenomenon which is a specific element of globalization dealing with this new transnational state. The governance of the European education policy space appears to be increasingly 'produced' through building relations between actors in networks and communities, which are themselves no longer contained within the silos and discourses of the national.

A Single Space? Comparison and Complexity

The governing project of European integration is fundamentally concerned with the construction of a single European space, a 'monotopia', capturing the idea of a one-dimensional (mono) discourse of a space and territory (topos) (Jensen & Richardson 2004). The single market and single currency are examples of a concerted attempt to create Europe as 'one space' by removing constraints to the physical movement of goods and people for the sake of mobility, accessibility and connectivity, which are seen as answers to social and economic problems like exclusion, peripherality and uncompetitiveness (Jensen & Richardson, 2004, pp. 223-224). However, Europe is also a heterotopia of different scales and sites, fluid and changing, mediated by language barriers, regional histories, and immovable national projects. It is itself swept by international pressures, political, financial, technological and cultural, and it is simultaneously located in and produced by the global, the idea of the European and the national. It is operating at different speeds: with high velocity and scale through a cosmopolitan cross-border elite, and with low velocity and local embeddedness in distant sectors.

The flow and reach of Europeanization is enhanced and shaped by the indicators and data produced in the construction of Europe as a legible, governable, commensurate policy space. This process is built upon the post-war creation of European (or Europe-based) associations of national research centres, networks of cosmopolitan researchers in education across Europe, and the growth of common projects, with useful comparative data and new research technologies. Comparison is a key element in the management of multinational companies and is dependent on numerical data: the scale, velocity and scope of the uses of numerical data to manage grow exponentially all the time. Comparison for constant improvement against competition has come to be the standard by which public systems are judged; indeed as the project of Europe is now judged. While states originally managed this process of comparison in a limited way, the flow of national data internationally has increased. Comparison is now cross-border; it is both an abstract form of competition and a proxy for other forms of rivalry. Comparison is highly visible as a tool of governing at all levels – at the level of the organization (to manage) and of the state (to govern). Comparison through indicators, benchmarking and ranking drives the Europeanization process forward today.

Nation-state understanding of places has provided a particular imagery of territoriality – boundedness, cohesion, social solidarity, functional integration of administrative levels – which still exerts a powerful influence on the way we think about European space (Nóvoa, 2000; Delanty & Rumford, 2005). On the other hand, there is a recognition that distinctly European spaces in different fields are emerging, but that the properties, dynamics and potential of these spaces are not sufficiently understood. To understand this emergent European space, new images have been introduced – networks, flows and scapes – all of which emphasize the fluidity, mobility and interconnectedness which are characteristic of contemporary Europe and the European policy space. What makes policy travel or flow across Europe, within wider policy spaces, is of interest here. What problems are solved in this way? What remains stubbornly resisting the external? What appears to flow but only thinly? What is used as camouflage, mimicry or mimesis? Our previous research reveals similarities and differences between national sites. More to the point, it has produced evidence of apparent travel and flow when there are only discursive simulacra, a common language but uncommon contexts. Processes of Europeanization are subdued or hidden within this complexity; they appear to be global, national and local at the same time. Where are Europe-wide processes, producing data standards, translating text, mediating meanings or agreeing exchanges, which enable flow to take place? What speeds up and what slows down policy exchange, and the concomitant elements (experts, data and technologies) that support or inhibit flow and comparison?

Governing through data, in systems created and expectant of older relations, is a major, new confusion while appearing as a simple, logical governing process. So Europeanization is both a harmonizing and a dislocating process. The EU as a new form of transnational cooperation has invented or sustained innovative forms of policy making across borders and novel forms of governance. The EU is in a process of constant agreement or dissension managed through hard regulation (precise, legally binding obligations) and forms of persuasion, or soft law. Europeanization is a delicate process and not a constant condition or state, moving between areas of defended national sovereignty and using new actors with new policy instruments in some policy areas.

Networks and Standards

The field of education as a new policy area has moved over the years from a small vocational training area and wider actions on a cultural Europe into an integrated policy of benchmarked improvement in which education is a comparable area of public policy. The growing ambitions about education in the EU, the political sensitivities which envelop it, and gradually consolidating overall policy goals, meant that it developed a distinctive style of governance. Although affected by different policy instruments (the open method of coordination, voluntary agreements, standard setting, networks), European governance in education has relied on the creation and consolidation of networks, often through projects or special funding, and on the creation of standards.

Networks and standards are of value because they work well with the soft governance of an emerging policy space: they are constantly in creation, both demanded and necessary yet voluntary and open. They operate like a mix of regulation and open source construction. Standards are dependent on network and data processes. They have not the fixedness of past times; they are rather fluid, relative and performance based. Standards bring into being actors and areas to be governed. They are a tool which is effective in European trading policy globally and which fits closely with the EU policy of soft governance. It is a lightly regulated, persuasive and self-managing form of governing in which standards depoliticize policy; soft governance relies on negotiation, persuasion and agreed performance and standardization uses an expertise which supports it. Standards fit with the contemporary problems of managing education/lifelong learning in Europe. The shaping and governing of the amorphous and less discernible field of education, a hybrid state of public and private actors, is a major task. The contrast between the cultural strategies of a constructed 'Europe', evolved from earlier national policies, and used as a deliberate policy of identity and mission construction, and the globalized space which increasingly flows across states, displacing educational discourses and meanings, is the point of focus for the problem of 'constructing the European Education Space' (Nóvoa & Lawn, 2002).

The gradual shift in governance in Europe to a regulated or steered space of learning via benchmarks and standards is part of a broad response to the complexity of tasks and the arrival of a thickening mesh of mobile private and public agents, working across borders, institutions and purposes. By the late 1990s, the European area of education policy involved a range of system administrators in national agencies, cities and regions and a growing range of actions in schools and higher education (exchanges, study tours, networks, teaching resources, etc.). In recent years, the rise of education as a key policy area in a knowledge economy, with the quality of education central to a competitive economy and international comparisons of educational productivity and performance, is easier to discern. The European Space for Education, in all its forms and possibilities, is emerging as a multifaceted web of relations, as commerce, technology-based networks, associations, intergovernmental relations and competition all act to drive it into existence. By its nature, as a transnational flow of information, it is being created in sharp contrast to the older central roles played by organizations, hard law, statist jurisdictions, rigid borders and national sites. Consequently, it is a disorientation as much as an ordering, as it flows around older 'sites' and works with new sites, networks and standards.

The Creation of the European Education Space

The apparent indeterminacy of the European Space should not disguise its transparency as a hypermodern form of effective governance, taking account of new knowledge shifts and rapidly absorbing their possibilities. It is easier to imagine it as multiple spaces, built around function and interest, operating at different intensities and levels, occupying innumerable areas and spheres. The emergence of soft law, open coordination, is intended to speed up and increase the effectiveness of the knowledge economy aim by benchmarking performance. It is an effective way of 'creating' Europe by 'creating' policy areas in its own new image. It is an attempt to find a form of effective governance, knitting together public and private sectors, and overcoming older national bordered systems. The emerging policy space of education in Europe, a process of complex, network governance, needs actors who take on the functions of governance, import and renew languages of 'external' agencies, become absorbed into policy arenas, and act on behalf of hybrid policy agendas. So, few actors engaging in 'European' networks are free agents; they have mobility but as they move, they are constructing and constructed by their engagement.

Rising free from older ideas of territory and people, Europe recognizes that a (transnational) state is a political and cultural project, an idea and a conduit, a projection and a form, in which meaning is created, delivered and maintained through governance. If meaning binds the state's forms and future, and shapes identity and systems, then the idea of Europe and the place of education are thrown into relief. Europe is not a place, a warehouse full of cultural artefacts, institutions and asymmetrical systems. Europe is a project, a space of meaning, a state in process, and education is a core technology in which governance, ordering and meaning can be constructed.

Europe as a fluid concept, shaping itself as it moves, needs a governing discourse by which its legitimacy and purpose can be determined. The revelation of a 'European education area' is fundamental to the contemporary structuring of the EU; it announces the arrival of a major discursive space, centred on education in which the legitimation, steering and shaping of European governance is being played out. It is a significant attempt to manage the launch of a new transnational state by producing an idea which links together education, work and citizenship as its 'big idea'. Like any governing discourse, it tries to discipline but it must also deliver meaning: a confidence in the project, a sense of future and a workable system.

The construction of the European Union has been marked by a perplexing silence around education policy. To students of the European constitution, politics and administration, this silence reflects the fact that education is not a significant policy area within the EU, except at the level of national systems, operating under the framework of the principle of subsidiarity. It has not been one of the main pillars of policy and is not relevant to the key arenas of regulation, law or trade. Yet this was always one of the paradoxes of the EU, for within national systems, education played a key role in stabilizing the state and aiding its reproduction, and 'education is, by definition, the space for the construction of national identity' (Nóvoa, 1996, p. 46). So, although the field of education has not featured greatly in discussions about Europeanization processes in the past, it is an interesting case, and one which is moving into prominence. It is an area which sits uneasily within regulation studies or even adaptive system thinking, yet it offers insights about how power is exerted in Europe in sophisticated ways; it is opaque and indirect and uses soft tools.

The European education area has gone through changes over time. Originally, the emphasis on education was intended to create a new cultural identity, creating a shared European imaginary. This was sustained by numerous projects, networks and thematic networks on cross-institutional collaboration or simple academic collaborations, emanating from the Directorate-General for Education and Culture, and its predecessors, in programmes such as Socrates, Leonardo and Comenius. In recent years, many national education experts have been working on European projects to do with equity, quality, investment in education, participation in lifelong learning and private expenditure on education and training. The need for documentation and statistics, in relation to the recognition of qualifications or benchmarking of progress since the Lisbon Summit in March 2000, has produced a change in the institutions of governance at the European level, for example, the influence of EuroStat, EuroBarometer or the European Education Thesaurus, and partnerships with international organizations, like the Organization for Economic Cooperation and Development (OECD) Programme for International Student Assessment (PISA) group. Under the auspices of the European Statistical System (ESS) a special task force on lifelong learning and statistical data (European Commission, 2001a) was created to bring together all the current demands for numerical information and indicators from within European programmes, and those demanded by new intentions for social and economic development (European Commission 2001b). In effect, education experts created the foundations for the 'calculative rationality' (Bauman, 1992) needed to create this Europeanization process in education. This combination of a higher profile education area, mutating into learning and linked to the knowledge economy aims, and structured through networking and benchmarking, is seen within the Commission as creating a European policy space in education; that is:

> The Lisbon conclusions implicitly give the Union the mandate
> to develop a common interest approach in education going
> beyond national diversities as can already be seen in the
> demand to Ministers of Education to debate common
> objectives of educational systems. This mandate will lead to
> an increase in the European dimension of national educational
> policies. (Hingel, 2001, pp. 15 & 19)

The series of meetings through which progress on achieving a dynamic economy will lead logically to a 'European Model of Education' (Hingel, 2001, p. 4) can be viewed within the Commission's annual reports of progress (European Commission, 2004b, 2005b).

A combination of steering mechanisms for lifelong learning, citizenship and the knowledge economy 'will reorder the (educational) site, widening the field, integrating its functions, centring the individual learner, stressing performance and comparing. Comparison will be easier after the landscape has been reordered and made transparent' (Lawn, 2003, p. 12). Assembling and governing this policy space in education is happening simultaneously. It is being assembled in the contemporary

European way, by construing it as a performance area, and managing it by indicators, benchmarks and comparison.

The Importance of 'Soft': networks, space and meaning

Our understanding of Europeanization processes is based on the effects of networks and actors in creating policy spaces; in the governing of education in Europe through persuasion and attraction, and the hidden politics of data and standards; and in the meaning provided by the European project. This approach will be discussed in more depth later (in chapter 4) but it allows a concentration on the work of actors – as partners, experts and participants – in the construction of Europeanizing projects and networks.

Supporting networks and involving experts has been the mainstay of European Commission policy, and the flows of people and the thick web of networks and communication have formed the space of education, through which the Commission shapes policy. Lifelong learning, citizenship and the knowledge economy are shaping and being shaped together as the determining characteristics of this space. In a way, this policy space is not just a place of work but, for some, an 'intellectual homeland' as well, a place of meaning making (Lawn, 2008). At the same time, the EU governs through these policy networks and spaces, providing European solutions to European problems.

Europeanization in education is being pursued through this mobilizing governance in which its subjects may be attracted to it through formal or less formal attempts to nurture support and meaning about it. It is a soft governance in which pedagogy, learning and education have come to represent a governing arena and a form of governing which is not statutory or nationally bounded. It is a mode of governance which is increasingly underpinned by, and measured through, data and standardization. Affinities can be created in the education arena through the professional space it offers across Europe, which associations and actors have used to generate new spaces for action and meaning. Experts work with an expertise which is portable. They act as points of distribution for the ideas of Europeanization, creating, imagining and transmitting, and existing within and outwith diverse steered partnerships. Significant system actors may also act as symbolic analysts (Reich, 1991), dealing with abstract Europeanization ideas in education policy, or building experimental or analytical policy networks. Europe, as an exchange of ideas, as a desirable state, as a place in which the new European imaginary is mutually constructed, works with the educationalists and professionals it engages and persuades.

The complex responses and positioning of these system actors, working on problems of harmonization, competition and exchange in European committees, in task force groups and other supranational bodies, showed them to be simultaneously observers, agents, translators, evaluators and even oppositionalists. They were crucial actors in the construction of this extra-national policy sphere. Interviewing them revealed the existence of a gradually emerging and distinctive European policy culture in education, constructed through a wide array of committees, exchanges, commissions, networks and regulations, in which they worked to use, shape and imagine a European education of the future. The urgencies and sensitivities of the system actors is displayed and circulated within new virtual and embodied sites of educational policy (not only national offices) and involve a progressing process negotiation and networking, creating and recreating a new culture of policy making, and progressively reconstructing its identity. (Lawn & Lingard, 2002, p. 290)

Concluding: main points of the argument

European education as a subject of inquiry began long before the European Union came into fruition. There was a trade in knowledge in different forms between people, cities, and universities in Europe in the past; states had permeable, national borders; and there was a transfer and exchange of ideas, practices and goods across their borders. Flows of technology, and their discourses, took place across intergovernmental regulation and standardization, in science, in comparative research and in modelling the future. For example, the post-war growth of powerful research institutions in education, at the national and at European level, enabled advanced technical and scientific competence to develop as a cross-European resource and then act as the foundation for the governing of education in Europe by data. The Europeanization of education refers to these constant processes and to the scale, speed and purposes brought to them by the EU, and produced what Janne, in 1973, called an 'irreversible initial movement towards an educational policy at European level'. This movement was built on the European ideal of cooperation, which develops into a distinctive governing approach in European education.

As Janne stated in his Report, 'Europeanization' should be understood as the creation of a 'normal space' so that teachers and researchers could move across it easily, and in a way, plant a new European flag in this frontier (Janne, 1973, p. 12). Europeanization had, and continues to have, its own European symbols, produced in favour of the new 'workable future' and initially, against 'le défi américain'.

Soft power is viewed here as the cultivation of support and the creation of meaning inside and around the idea of a European Union, and its relation to the field of education in particular. It was developed to shape a space of meaning in a fuzzy Europe, and to reflect the idea of a cooperative space. As voluntarism and agreement was one element, another was expertise and partnership. Supporting networking by projects was a continued effort to build an enhanced 'normal' space.

Europe is imagined as a 'community of ourselves' in EU policy documents and this is still present even in the panoptic envisioning of European governance which has grown today. The integration and adaptation of political systems is not sufficient to explain new European spaces of shared meanings, and the production of common purposes and identities. Space is reconfigured constantly as the new policy spaces – city to city networks, peripheral countries, cross-border associations, horizontal networks – work with each other across multiple centres. However, networks, projects and associations have all had to overcome the problems of knowing 'where they are'; new ways of organizing across Europe; establishing communicative spaces; sharing work; supporting collegiality. The idea of the platform, a viewpoint and a base for communication, essential for the construction of a 'home' in the space, is not easy for the network.

European governance represents a shift from hierarchy and state hierarchies, and uses sets of institutions and actors that are drawn from, but also beyond, government. The legitimacy of governing authority cannot be demanded but has to be negotiated and its relation with its partners in civil society is one of steering, guiding and contracting. Today, its experts, drawn from all over Europe, are engaged in producing new European standards on learning platforms, indicators or school quality, which will become interoperable or consistent across Europe. They circulate an explicit language of comparison and evaluation, new generic skills and 'learning' which, although of wider international usage than specifically 'European', appear in particular forms in the Europeanizing space. Governing this space occurs not just by agents, data, discourse or regulation, but also by standards. But soft governance offers a lightly regulated, persuasive and self-managing form of governing in which policy is depoliticized and invites new hosts into its voluntary activities. 'Light-touch', optional, economical and effective are its features. While its effects are significant and ordering, the process may be delicate, and the discourse 'soft'.

In the twenty-first century, the European policy space has been driven by data and standards as well as networking. The role of the OECD in framing and steering education policy, and the way in which PISA constitutes an important node in the complex task of governing European education, is an outward sign of the growth of data and its production by European agencies (Grek, 2009). Increasingly, the data these agencies collected, analysed and combined have become part of a significant change in the governing of Europe. Earlier aims, to do with spreading information, have become overshadowed by their critical importance of comparison and benchmarking in governing Europe. The new 'missionaries of our time' travel with and translate their 'data dream' of infinite interoperability across the education policy space in Europe (and beyond).

CHAPTER 2

Research and Policy in European Education: the first stage

Europe in Competition

European education as a subject of inquiry began before the European Union came into fruition, and early expertise and data in this area became the foundation for the EU's research in educational policy.

The relation between each nation-state and its neighbours across Europe has been a constant feature since the growth of national education systems and all their necessary service and system parts in the nineteenth century. No national system of education developed in isolation, removed from all contamination of technologies and ideas, and pursuing its own particular path. Indeed, these education systems were often formed as a means of national pride or competition with neighbours, and in direct knowledge of other ways of achieving improvements. While operating within the vernacular, and being inscribed as such by political actors, they operated within a wider world. This was the European past in education just as much as it is a continuing element within the EU.

This sense of a wider European context is absent from those national histories of course, so that they often appear to be clear of all influence apart from the national – the important Education Law or Act, the crucial agency of state, the famous professor and university, the determining influence of the long-established journal. Historians of education, the scribes of the national, and comparativists, the scholars of the relational national, have tended to produce constructed silos of the national and use law, identity and character as descriptors of it. Sometimes, European events disrupt this narrative; sometimes a footnote in the text refers to a cross-border influence, or a climactic political shift is referred to only as a decision to change the textbook or school system. Generally speaking, education (schooling) existed within national narratives and it rarely helped the case, the construction of the nation and the state, to imply an external influence, drawn from another, sometimes rival, society.

Yet it is an error in the process of understanding European education to confuse place with space, and territory with the imagined community of ideas and practices, which these examples demand. European education started before the 1992 Maastricht Treaty, often seen as the start of the drive to Europeanize education. There was a trade in ideas, designs and knowledge between people, cities and universities in Europe in the past; states had permeable national borders; and there was a relocation, transfer and exchange of ideas, practices and goods across their borders. Understanding the contemporary European policy space in education must begin with its recent past. It continues to reflect continuing themes in the relation between the national and the transnational.

During the nineteenth century European societies were constructing their education systems and everything in them – desks, textbooks, wall charts, school design and teacher training. At the same time, they were displaying their innovations and educational goods in world exhibitions or being observed by travelling researchers. So, from the earliest days, educational systems were being materially or discursively influenced through their permeable borders. It wasn't just proximity or curiosity which drove these influences, but economic competition, and France, Germany and the United Kingdom were at the forefront of this European activity. Competition was also at the heart of cooperation, as international standards and classifications became the subject of a series of nineteenth-century congresses in many areas of communication and industry, and so, even in education.

The role of world exhibitions in the nineteenth and early twentieth centuries was to put European nations into an elevated, viewable space. They linked the national and local with the international and global. Nationalism and internationalism are in tension in the space, and so is the relation between government, business and media. It was a dimension of European education which illuminates classifications and genealogies, networks and audiences, cross-border industries of education, and the factors which shape discursive and technical exchanges. Exhibitions were not stand-alone events; they shaped cultural and social institutions and practices within borders but also across them. People were drawn to see them and returned with new ideas. Exhibitions produced documents, brochures and images through which the ephemeral was turned into reference material. The actuality of the objects, their captions, their displays and systems were imbued with the rules of classification, and became circulated as part of the international industry of education, used in museums and classrooms.

Exhibitions acted as catalysts within the formation of national education systems. In this early form of comparison in education, it was the representations of systems, particularly key objects, and ideas of national identity, that were compared and this information was extrapolated back into statements about national progress across Europe. Objects ('things') symbolized modern education above all else. For example, in 1902 Michael Sadler, Director of the Office of Special Inquiries and Reports in the UK Board of Education, included research reports produced for a world exhibition in his Office reports. Vol. 8, Special Report included a Report on Education in Norway, Education in Sweden, Primary, Secondary and Technical Education in Portugal, and Education in Serbia, which had all been produced by their own governments for the Paris Exhibition of 1900. In this way, a strong sense of Europe as an interlinked territory, through trade, ideas and systems, was created, just as much as one in which diversity and difference were reinforced.

The nineteenth and early twentieth centuries have accounts of travellers, sometimes official, sometimes not, moving across borders and into new educational landscapes, observing and recording them, and returning home to report. The most famous was Horace Mann's journey across Europe, and especially to Scotland and Prussia. Travel is associated with the clarification of judgements, vicarious knowledge, and a curiosity about alternative practices and solutions. Mann's travel was the first of a growing wave inside Europe. For example, in the late nineteenth century, a book was produced in London on school architecture. It was a response to a particular circumstance – the urgent need to build new schools, following the first national Education Act, for the London School Board. It was a direct response by a responsible officer to a governing need, by travelling to known sites of good practice in Europe.

> Robson brought together for his readers in one space, designs
> from across Europe and America. He assembled knowledge
> from widely dispersed sites and juxtaposed them in new
> combinations, which offered the reader opportunities for
> reflection, comparison and judgment. Robson's book also
> represents the movement of knowledge from the particularities
> of its site of production to a wider community of interested
> observers – a school built in Berlin to a particular philosophy
> of education is described, drawn, explained as a functioning
> design and included in his published gazetteer of school
> architecture and thereby transferred as a 'commodity' to other
> audiences. (Burke & Grosvenor, 2007, pp. 39-54)

The relation between the traveller and governing education is an open one and capable of interpretation but its possibilities include the traveller as an agent of the conscious or unconscious transfer of ideas or objects, of translation (a process of mediation) or trade (an act of exchange) (Ydesen, 2012). This kind of 'travel' became associated with the rise of specialist centres which accumulated and translated reports from elsewhere and sometimes sent out their own travellers; for example, the (English) Board of Education Department of Special Inquiries, in the late nineteenth century, produced major volumes on European education:

Volume I. 1897. Education in England, Wales and Ireland, France, Germany, Denmark, Belgium.
Volume II. 1898. Education in England and Wales. Physical Education. The Heuristic Method of Teaching. University Teaching in France.
Volume III. 1898. National Organisations of Education in Switzerland. Secondary Education in Prussia, Baden and Sweden. Teaching of Modern Languages. Higher Commercial Education in France, Germany and Belgium.
Volume VII. 1902. Rural Education in France.
Volume VIII. 1902. Education in Scandinavia, Switzerland, Holland, Hungary.
Volume IX. 1902. Education in Germany.

The International Institute at Teachers College, New York, from 1900 to 1940, became a nodal point of information about education systems, a publisher of reports and articles, and official evaluator for government-sponsored inquiries.

The ideas, system components and technologies which moved across the European landscape are the foundation events which underpin the construction of the European education space today. Wandering folk of ideas, like Montessori or Decroly or Grundtvig, may then be placed back inside the right frame – not just famous national figures but educationalists across European frontiers. Although their work is created in particular places, its influences moves across and between these places through the actions of individuals and the exporting of pedagogical practices and tools.

Advanced students of education, studying for degrees not available at home, travel across Europe and often in Germany. In the forested areas of Thuringia, in Germany, lies the important university city of Jena. Its importance lies in its place in the philosophical, literary and national history of Germany. However, at the turn of the last century, Jena was the place to study the works of Herbart and the new pedagogy of education, not only across Germany but across Europe. It has been said that a third of the students in the university in the first decade of the twentieth century were studying with Professor Rein, the great interpreter of Herbart, and travelling back to their own countries to spread the practices of the new educational sciences. For example, in Edinburgh and later Manchester, the work of Rein was passed on and many of the early professors of education in the United Kingdom were ex-pupils of

Rein at postgraduate level. They had to learn German to pass their advanced coursework and were often at ease in later years, reading and writing German texts. The history of education sciences in Europe began with this kind of shared theory and practice and was carried back and forth by Jena's ex-students, for example. Geneva, the Swiss city almost surrounded by France, was from the 1920s a major site of study for students from all over Europe, who came to a strong base of the new progressive education at the Institut Jean Jacques Rousseau, under its Directors, Claparede and Bovet. It was one of the sites of work of the new European version of progressive education, the New Education Fellowship, which had a series of influential conferences across Europe in the 1920s and the 1930s.

During the twentieth century, Europe was a web of communications and routes, linking sites and individuals, a web increasing in density and complexity. It had several features. There was a particular form of supply and demand in the sphere of education and its services across Europe; this viewed educational products such as specialist languages, particular practices or technology, specific training programmes, tests or textbooks which were created for local markets as exportable. These products flowed to new markets, via commerce, travellers, competition and innovative educational actors. This was not the dominant way of describing vernacular systems, nor could it be when the nation-state defended its practices as quintessentially national. But it was a cross-European effect.

Mid-Twentieth-Century European Research Formation

The formation of the nascent European Space for Education was founded on mid-century, and particularly post-war, networks of experts, researchers and policy actors, who came together in new national and then European centres and institutions working in education. The disrupted work of the 1930s resurfaced in the late 1940s in Western European states reconstructing their inadequate education systems, and trying to either expand their selective secondary education or devise a new comprehensive model. New transnational institutions, based in Europe, depended on linking together the newly established national centres and their expertise. The 1950s saw the emergence of a new European idealism in which education was featured.

Research Projects

European researchers are more and more able to engage in pan-European research projects of different kinds today, funded through the European Union and national agencies and foundations. But in the early twentieth century, cross-European projects were much more unusual. Scientific congresses, the growth of the New Education Fellowship conferences and sponsored visits to other country's education systems were developing an elite of cosmopolitan educationalists, aware of other ideas and practices, and scientific results published elsewhere. Professors of education were few in number but often they had knowledge of each other, due to common language use and book and journal publishing.

In the field of education, the growth of national research centres, of various kinds, their collaborations and their involvement in European projects have been and continue to be crucial in the process of a transnational European policy space. National centres began to develop in the early 1930s and then again in the 1950s. One of the first major European projects, which joined together professors, statisticians, head teachers, and policy activists, was the International Examinations Inquiry, a scientific project, well funded by the Carnegie Corporation in New York, operating from 1931 to 1938, which undertook significant exchanges of data that focused on the pressing policy problem of the selection of pupils for their elite secondary education systems. It comprised key research figures and centres in the USA, Scotland, England, France, Germany and Switzerland, and then included Norway, Sweden and Finland, with a large core of members and a wider group of national participants. It produced a series of significant publications on examinations and intelligence. It is the first solid example of a new form of Europeanization. It involved approximately one hundred leading researchers across Europe, at a time when they were scarce in number. It defined a common problem, clarified terms, engaged in critical discussion, jointly produced and managed a series of linked projects and published its work internationally. It appears to model or at least foreshadow a spate of post-Second World War international studies and the establishing of common epistemic communities, in which loosely integrated professional, academic and policy actors were networked across borders.

The major comparative educationalists of their day worked in this project, Sadler, Monroe and Kandel; it was Kandel who explained the value of the project for the future:

> educational systems … as different as those of pre- Nazi Germany, France, England, Scotland, Norway, Sweden, Finland, and the United States, could work together on one important educational problem which was woven into the fabric of their educational systems. The international study of examinations, which was conducted from 1931 to 1938 showed how a common attack could be made on a common problem without imposing uniformity on any of the participating nations. It demonstrated clearly that the problem of examinations had to be solved from within a national system of education and that international co-operation in its

solution did not mean any imposition from without. (Kandel, 1955, p. 7)

There are few straight lines between the work of experts and centres in Europe in the 1930s and the post-war foundation of the new Europe, but there are connections. With common funding, they worked on a single policy problem, common to European education systems, even if it was often seen as a national problem, the problem of selection for an expanding secondary education. The project worked on a cutting-edge scientific and policy frontier – testing, examining and standardizing in the selection process. In their own countries, the Inquiry members are the early pioneers of educational research in its different forms – the study of intelligence testing, comparisons between national systems, promoters of the new child-based pedagogy – and they are all pioneers in the sense that they were working internationally. A consequence of this work is that a cosmopolitan elite group of European educational researchers was created, with reputations crossing borders and group members often travelling and studying in other countries. It also resulted in the close linking of national research centres across European borders and the 'internationalization' of research theories and methodologies, particularly in statistics in education. Isaac Kandel proposed this project as a model for European cooperation in education and recommended it as the exemplar for the post-war United Nations Educational, Scientific and Cultural Organization (UNESCO), for which he was an adviser. He represented the comparativist's view at the time that

> Without doing more than promoting discussions and publishing reports, UNESCO can at least bring before the profession of education and the public opinions from different national sources on the educational issues of the day. And among the most important of these issues is that of the content and methods of promoting international understanding and cooperation, not as something to be superimposed on national curricula and courses but to be woven naturally into them, (1955, p. 14)

Developing European Research Institutions and Skills

Torsten Husén, the Swedish quantitative researcher, and a leading example of the new post-war emergence of a European class of education researchers, laid out the new version of comparative education which would work with educational planners, who were coming into their own in Europe in the 1950s:

> The willingness of educational planners, a new breed of the mid-twentieth century, to learn from other colleagues in other countries goes far beyond what their predecessors (whatever

they are called) in the era of Auslandspedagogik were ready to take in. Under such auspices comparative education as a new field of academic inquiry was born.

Educational research has also transgressed national confines. Scientific research in general, not least in the natural sciences, has always been international in character, given its ambition to discover principles and facts with universal validity. Research in education, however, for a long time lacked universalistic ambitions, simply because of the unique or particular features of the country and the national system of education where the researchers were based. (Husén, 1983, p. 24)

From the 1950s, and based in western Europe, in Hamburg and Paris, new European (later international) institutions were established covering the main areas of education and immediately pulling together key policy actors and research specialists.

UNESCO and the Comparativists

The 5th UNESCO General Conference, in June 1950, instructed the Director-General to find the funds for the creation of UNESCO Centres in Germany from private sources or Member States. In the Director-General's report submitted to the next General Conference in summer 1951 plans were put forward to establish three 'special projects': a Centre for International Youth Work, an Institute for Social Sciences, and an Institute for Education. They were intended to help tackle some of the fundamental problems, sociological, psychological and pedagogical, which bear upon the relations between the German people and more particularly German youth and other nations. The Institute for Education established an international governing board mainly from representatives of the occupying Western powers. Famous names such as Jean Piaget, Karl Stern and Maria Montessori joined the Board. It opened in the summer of 1952. In its first mainly European phase, in the 1950s and early 1960s, UNESCO, through its new Institute for Education, with its new journal, the *International Review of Education*, drew together scholars and researchers in comparative education which enabled the growing international policy links to be established. It acted as an information centre, a node, for educational research and policy in Europe. It reported on inquiries into compulsory schooling, teacher education, the teaching of reading and writing, and adult education. It produced a World Survey of Education, a statistical overview of education around the world, and published *Education Abstracts*, ten times a year in English, French and Spanish.

The early UNESCO, based in Hamburg, drew together and published influential comparative educationalists – like Kandel and

Hans – to develop the case for it, so useful in the early days of EU education policy, that it was important to analyse and compare educational systems and the factors that determine and shape them, and to stress the principle of adaptation to different systems.

The International Association for the Evaluation of Educational Achievement (IEA) and Surveys

The formation of UNESCO, the founding of the Hamburg Institute and the continuing creation of national research centres or commissions in Europe (United Kingdom, Denmark, Norway, Sweden, Belgium, Finland, German Federal Republic) meant that research collaboration and joint work became synonymous with European cooperation.

> IEA was founded at a historical turning point in the history of educational research. In the decade after the Second World War, a definite willingness of governments to support and utilize research in education appeared in the belief that the studies would be useful to the formulation and conduct of educational policy. Government agencies turned to research workers for 'answers' to what was considered to be basically the 'scientific' problems involved in planning educational reforms. Policy-orientated research increased rapidly. The 'Plowden Committee' in Great Britain, the 'Bildungsrat' in the Federal Republic of Germany, and the 'School Commission' in Sweden, are cases in point. (Landsheere, n.d., p. 8)

New university institutes of educational research were founded and the staffs of existing ones increased. Ministries of education set up departments concerned with research and planning, which either commissioned policy-oriented research from the universities or from independent research institutes, or even undertook it themselves. Institutes, special commissions, research centres and linked experts began to work regularly across western Europe.

In the 1950s, educational researchers from different countries met regularly, particularly at the UNESCO Institute for Education, Hamburg, to examine common policy problems, for example, with school structures and organization, selection processes, examinations and school failure, and to devise ways of investigating education systems comparatively empirically. These meetings became the basis for one of the most influential of the new European associations, working across policy and research, the International Association for the Evaluation of Educational Achievement (IEA). It undertook its first study in part to see whether it was possible and meaningful to carry out large-scale cross-European projects, which became more international later as more national centres joined. In the first stage, in 1960, research centres from

Belgium, England, Finland, France, Germany, Israel, Poland, Scotland, Sweden, Switzerland, the United States and Yugoslavia took part. By 1962, and with a significant US grant, other countries joined. It was coordinated from the UNESCO Institute in Hamburg. Beginning with a study of school mathematics, through tests and questionnaires, it provided the template for later studies on Science, French and English as foreign languages, Reading Comprehension, Literature and Civic Education. The aim of this type of survey research was to examine the relationships between the 'outcomes' of educational systems and a series of data on the 'input' to the systems both within and between countries.

The effect of this steered collaboration was to enhance and stabilize powerful research institutions in education across Europe and to develop advanced technical and scientific competence as a cross-European resource. It had the further effect of making systems more transparent to the national policy makers and across Europe. Ways of measuring complex variables in education systems also have the effect of aiding their shape and direction.

> There is no doubt that IEA had a very substantial influence on the development of educational research activities in all the countries that it has involved in any way, particularly in those countries where, previously, education research efforts had been of small extent and sophistication. Overall, this influence has been highly beneficial, resulting in the professionalization of educational personnel in the area of educational achievement measurement, statistical analysis of data, and the management of large scale educational projects. Again, it can be said that these developments would have had minimal likelihood of occurring without the existence of IEA. This was partly because IEA had to develop, in different countries, cadres of educational researchers that could help carry out IEA's investments. (Carroll, 1994, quoted in Landsheere, n.d., p. 9)

Like the International Examinations Inquiry in the 1930s, this movement of European researchers was partly founded on American money and involved American expertise. Again like the International Examinations Inquiry, it had strong links with Teachers College, Columbia, but also with Benjamin Bloom in Chicago. Increasingly it became closely linked with overseas experts as well.

> During more than three decades of existence, IEA has developed an extraordinary co-operative research and evaluation network world wide. IEA can identify and mobilize this network to review, plan, and assess how school systems are performing, how, why, and under what conditions education makes a difference. The benefits for universities and

for educational systems are considerable. (Landsheere, n.d., p. 7)

Certain educational policies which came to the fore in the 1960s, such as provisions for greater equality of educational opportunity, bilingual education, and the education of the disabled, could not have been properly framed and achieved without information provided by surveys and evaluation studies.

The IEA is one of the key examples of a new European collaboration, prefiguring the expert and policy underpinning of the current policy space, but there were others.

The Council of Europe set up committees dealing with research and development in education and the institutional conditions for research. Since the 1970s, the Centre for Research and Innovation (CERI) at the OECD brought officials and professors of education together in working and publishing groups, and in projects on new subjects, such as recurrent education.[1] (Husén, 1983, p. 27)

The International Institute for Educational Planning (IIEP) and Educational Statistics

In 1963, UNESCO (with the cooperation of the World Bank, the Ford Foundation and the French Government) established in Paris the International Institute for Educational Planning. Although the IIEP was mainly concerned with development education, its focus was on a new idea to Europe; that educational systems were an integral part of national, economic and social development and had become an essential 'investment expenditure' for economic growth (Coombs, 1970, p. 22). The IIEP took an important European issue: the explosive increase in popular demand for education (Coombs, 1970, p. 23) and the difficulties in managing the shift from an elite to a mass education system (Coombs, 1970, p. 24).

Educational planning was a relatively new idea and needed a community of scholars to push forward research and research training (Coombs, 1966, p. 24). At the same time, there was no organized body of knowledge on educational planning, and interdisciplinarity was essential. Gradually, the IIEP became a centre of expertise and networked knowledge and dissemination (Coombs, 1970, p. 48). Increasingly, it depended on statistical skills and methodologies, using expertise in North America and Europe, and created seminars drawing together professors of educational planning (statistics), professors of statistics and methodologies and other experts from universities and training organizations. It studied the types of statistical data needed for educational planning, the practical process of collecting such data, the methods of utilizing such data for planning purposes, and methods of teaching this material to students of educational planning (Coombs, 1966, pp. 336-337).

Alongside this accumulation of statistical expertise, the IIEP began to focus on complex questions about the quality of education; that is, how does one judge the quality of performance of an educational system? (Coombs, 1966, p. 342). An interdisciplinary symposium in June 1966 examined the different ways of measuring and assessing quality, and its relation to educational planning. Increasingly, the IIEP began to research and work upon a new version of planning:

> The aim must be to improve the performance of educational
> systems through changes that will make them more relevant to
> the needs of their clients, more efficient in their use of
> available resources, and a more effective force for individual
> and social development. (Coombs, 1970, p. 54)

By the early 1970s, the IIEP began to push forward the idea of education system indicators which would reveal what was happening within the system and between the system and its environment, and thus in the output and effectiveness of the system. For example, these indicators could reveal trends in the distribution of the teaching staff by age, qualifications, salary levels and years of service, changes in class size in various parts of the system, and in teaching hours.

> What constitutes the desirable minimum of indicators of this
> sort will depend *on* what is necessary and feasible in each
> situation; the more sophisticated the educational system, the
> more extensive its management information system can be.
> But even the simplest and least developed educational system
> – or individual school or university – will find it very worth
> while to know much more about itself than it has ever known
> before. (Coombs, 1970, pp. 58-59)

In this way, the IIEP drew together, across European borders, professors of education who had the skills it needed or could acquire them. It created a new community of researchers with the skills required to plan and evaluate education systems. It developed or translated the idea of the indicator, crucial in the later development of the EU, and policy actors and experts who could use them.

The way that national actors shifted into European forums and institutions in the post-war period is an important element in the development of European networking and pools of expertise. At the same time, as we have seen in the Hamburg meeting, they were beginning to find ways of linking together. Key scientific/policy individuals became personally known to each other, rather than through their publications. An exemplar of this kind of new European networking at this time was

Torsten Husén, a major education researcher in Sweden and its first professor of applied education research in Stockholm in the1950s. By the late 1950s, he had already become part of the Hamburg group, which emerged as the IEA, and an expert in changes in post-war German education, and as a consultant to the American administration, had visited the USA several times. With close colleagues, he worked with a major Swedish Commission on comprehensive education on its content, methods and ways of comparing pupil achievement.

So, at the same time that there was growing governmental recognition of the value of strong links between educational research and educational reform policies, and a consequent increase in funding, experts like Husén became useful and found opportunities for work elsewhere in Europe. Husén became a major expert and ubiquitous figure in the seminars and consultancies of UNESCO, the IIEP and the OECD, as well as crucial to the IEA. He was both a technical expert and a policy advisor. Necessary sites of production of educational ideas, tools and products across Europe were studied apart from the flows and effects of technology, individuals or discourses associated with them, except within specialist or national narratives of context. These studies took place in intergovernmental regulation and standardization, in science and in comparative research.

The Idea of a Common Project

In the twentieth century, the relations between education sites began with the invention, publication and exchange of scientific production and scientists, and the training of advanced researchers. The establishment of a European education project realized its own early journal in *Paedagogica Europaea*, later the *European Journal of Education*. This was originally funded by the European Cultural Foundation (ECF) and the European Commission; the ECF was an independent foundation which, from 1968 to 1975, had a major project on European science: one of its four areas was Education, chaired by Janne. The ECF's Institute of Education in Paris began to publish the journal from 1979. According to its first editor, 'Our main purpose is to help forward the integration of European education by bringing together the work of those who are developing education, whether as administrators, as teachers, or as investigators' (Lloyd, 1964, p. 223).To do this, the *Paedagogica Europaea* needed to know:

> (i) how do we organize internationally the exchange of research information, while the work is in progress?
> (ii) how do we circulate quickly and certainly to the expert researchers in different countries the ascertained results of investigations?

(iii) how do we circulate among key people in different countries in administrative and executive positions in national and local education a comprehensible account of the research that is relevant to people responsible for running schools and universities etc? (Notes of a talk given at Frankfurt, 6 February 1964 [Lloyd, 1964, pp. 221-222])

Janne Report

When Henri Janne (1973) produced his report, *For a Community Policy on Education*, a milestone in thinking about a policy, he wanted to question European citizens who were engaged with 'educational experiments of significance for the future in Community countries' (p. 6). Naturally, he turned towards the experts and institutions which existed inside Europe: the IIEP, CERI, OECD, Council of Europe, UNESCO, Conference of European Rectors and the IEA.

Janne summed up the policy and administrative context in 1973; after listing a series of small-scale but growing actions, a new and organic link made between education and scientific policy in the Commission, and the closeness between education and the economy, he stated that

This complex constitutes, however, the irreversible recognition of an educational dimension of Europe and the irreversible initial movement towards an educational policy at European level. (1973, p. 10)

Although the report covers important ground for the later development of the EU, including a policy on permanent or recurrent education, and in culture and education, it focused directly on the relations with other international organizations 'in order to avoid unjustified duplication and the dissipation of effort' (Janne, 1973, p. 22).

Hoping that a proposed 'European Centre for Educational Development' was to be established by the Commission, the report proposed that it should deal with 'statistics (to be made comparable), information, educational research, the exchange of experiences etc. (Janne, 1973, p. 38) and databanks (p. 44), and it would discriminate between what the OECD/CERI could do and what it needed to do. One of its strategies would be to develop and work with university consortia, and to create centres of excellence for the Community which would work on specific and focused areas of policy.

After working through the range of necessary actions which Europe should take in relation to cultural policy, mobility and permanent education, the report stressed again the need for research:

In any event educational policy in Europe requires at least the setting up of a powerful Information centre covering all aspects of this vast field. But once again, to which organization

should it be linked? Communities? OECD? Council of Europe?
Should it be an organ sui generis? On any assumption,
experience indicates that up to date and complete information
is the raw material of any efficient policy and saves sometimes
extremely heavy expenses resulting from duplicated effort or
insufficient knowledge of what has been done or is being
done. (Janne, 1973, p. 59)

In its Resolution of 9 February 1976, three years later, the ministers of
education, working with the basis of the Janne Report, produced an
Action Programme, one of whose topics was 'the compilation of up to
date documentation and statistics on education' (Pépin, 2006). By 1980,
it had established CEDEFOP (the European Centre for the Development
of Vocational Training) (in 1975), to develop and coordinate research in
its field, and EURYDICE, a central information unit, mainly working
with national authorities, a Statistics office (Eurostat), and networks of
experts.(European Commission [EC], 1982, pp. 18-24). In addition, it
collaborated closely 'with the international organizations concerned with
educational problems and particularly with the Council of Europe, the
OECD and UNESCO (EC, 1979, p. 7).

Conclusion

The foundation of the European education policy from the 1970s
depended on much that had been in prior existence. It benefited from
national research centres and researchers who had begun to work
together from the 1950s in Europe; it benefited from their subjects of
study, and their quantitative and qualitative research expertise; it used
pre-existing institutions to work with and to model its own practices. As
an EU education policy began to emerge strongly, simply in the 1970s,
and then with some force in the late 1990s, it could rely on the research
work which preceded it – in comparing education systems, in cross-
border comparative research, and the reconceptualization of education
problematics, including the new field of permanent education or lifelong
learning which it has made its own – and the continuing networks and
associations of researchers.

The pressing problem of the 1990s was to overcome what Fragnière
could call the chaotic uniformity of European education, and the
necessity to create a European research infrastructure and policy, which
education policy desperately needed:

it appears that a European policy in education is in many
respects still to be invented ... Not only are the issues not yet
well defined but they are not mature enough for constituting
the object of thorough analysis or constructive developments
... what could be undertaken and achieved is a complete

construction, ... because of different sources and different definitions, figures often vary from one source to another. In Europe we have, therefore, a kind of chaotic uniformity, in the sense that while pretending to be uniform, even international organizations give quite different results. (Fragnière, 1979, pp. 311-312)

CHAPTER 3

Chaotic Uniformity: the rise of the European dimension in education, 1970-2000

It took some time for an economic community, originally focused on coal and steel, to work towards educational activity and even policy, although it should not then be surprising that its first steps were made in vocational education. Nor should it be surprising that as it evolved into a wider Community, and with a concern for identity and polity, that cultural and education policy were linked and developed. Education policy in Europe might be characterized as weak and even invisible within European Community studies but it did have a consistency from its days in the 1970s. It was always a sensitive issue. Ministers of education meeting together did not promote any action which would appear to be interference in their sacrosanct national domains. A European dimension in education tended to be ignored by the ministers and promoted by a small Commission enclave. It was a good idea which without funding or powerful agents seemed to lie dormant or be too weak to grow.

Yet there is a growing consistency from the 1970s onwards in this new policy dimension, which culminated in the mid to late 1990s in funded programmes which produced actions which echo back down the decades. The 1990s produced programmes which did not begin anew but built upon previous discourses about and action in education and its European dimension. The key governing idea through this time is cooperation, initially taken as a weak response to national sensitivity and then growing into a distinctive governing approach in European education. This chapter deals with education policy and action in this period and shows how there is a continuing purpose and a particular solution to its development.

The earliest element of educational policy at the Community level was vocational education, in its various guises as retraining, professional training, movement of workers across borders and an early Community consolidation around mutual recognition of qualifications. In 1963 the European Council adopted a decision establishing the 10 general principles for the development of a common vocational training policy. It did not give a strict definition of vocational training, thus allowing for broader interpretation (which would eventually include higher education) (Pépin, 2006, p. 56). But a common policy meant, in this case, not Community-level policy but an encouragement to action and a so-called responsibility by each Member State to enact the policy. However, millions of ECU were used to fund vocational training in the following decade.

Although this is a policy strand consistent with the creation of a market, it is not until the late 1970s that recognizable educational elements were created. The idea of Community cooperation in education was mentioned in 1971 when the six ministers of education first met. The Commission asked Professor Janne to formulate the first principles of an educational policy at Community level. Possible areas for cooperation were identified by Janne, a former Belgian Minister of Education, in the report he produced for the Commission in 1973:

> We understand by the term 'Europeanization' that the latter
> can conceive their recruitment of teachers, research workers
> and students, and their equipment – in a word, their policy
> and initiatives – 'as if' the Europe of the Nine constituted their
> normal space, after the style of the great American universities
> in their vast national territory. (Janne, 1973, p. 12)

Janne's report stressed the point that education was about fundamental values and was, therefore, a crucial part of cultural policy; although there were many cultural exchanges across Europe, there was no 'systematic promotion and coordination at Community level' (p. 12) and as a consequence, no close coordination with an educational policy referred to as a dialectical relationship. Also, the beginning of a scientific policy in 1972 was connected, by Janne, to education policy, particularly university advanced teaching and research, and permanent education (lifelong learning) (p. 13). Janne reflected the political position prevalent at the time – that 'national structures and educational traditions must be respected', autonomy must be valued and there must be a clear definition of the roles the Community intends to confer 'on the other international organizations' (p. 22). The problem of developing a forward plan or a strategy for education was bound about by the sensitivities around national autonomies. However, Janne proposed a number of possibilities around a European dimension in education; on exchanges, on knowledge of languages, on university consortia; on cooperation to create comparable data, and on educational research (p. 38). Permanent education was not only seen as a necessity for the new European economy but as a 'building site where little work has so far been done and which, in addition, would lead the Community to draw conclusions on educational policy in general' (p. 41).

There were concerns about this policy creating a European nationalism – a determined cross-border effect, a new imperialism – and during the 1980s there was a fear in the Community that in education policy, using a soft law approach, there was a gradual sovereignty transfer towards Brussels and the new international organizations based in Europe where the national is defined by a chauvinism which rejects any possibility of foreign intervention. And:

> In any event educational policy in Europe requires at least the setting up of a powerful Information Centre covering all aspects of this vast field. But once again, to which organization should it be linked? Communities? OECD? Council of Europe? Should it be an organ *sui generis*? On any assumption, experience indicates that up-to-date and complete information is the raw material of any efficient policy and saves sometimes extremely heavy expenses resulting from duplicated effort or insufficient knowledge of what has been or is being done.
> (Janne, 1973, p. 59)

The mid 70s push on the idea of a People's Europe and a sense of European citizenship specifically focused on school curricula as a means of developing a political education about Europe. Sensitivities in this area led to meetings of the European ministers of education being cancelled for a couple of years (Beukel, 2001, p. 129):

> it appears that a European policy in education is in many respects still to be invented. Not only are the issues not yet well defined but they are not mature enough for constituting the object of thorough analysis or constructive development.
> (Fragnière, 1979, p. 311)

And with regard to higher education statistics:

> because of different sources and different definitions, figures often vary from one source to another. In Europe we have, therefore, a kind of chaotic uniformity (Fragnière, 1979, p. 312)

Even in the late 1970s, it was still hard to discern something which could be called a European education policy or an arena in which it could exist. The weakness of actions taken and the lack of a commonality were due to the absence of a steering process and to a watchful concern of Member States over encroachments on their interests. Ministers of education, in 1975 and 1976, wished to discriminate between harmonization in economic and social policies, and diversity and tradition in education systems (Smith, 1980, p. 81)

37

> Phrases such as 'to take account of' or 'complementary to the national' were used to continue divergent practices. In the author's view, a European policy for teacher education would not be possible because that policy is at the heart of a nation's cultural identity and a 'key component of a nation's process of self renewal'. (Gwyn, 1979, p. 366)

But the fact that the Community had some funding and was becoming an active agent began to create effects:

> on European policy) a significant (if little publicised) intensification at grassroots level in institutions of higher education, complemented by beginnings of programmes, national and European, designed to respond to them ... these are characterised by academic motivation, recognition of new realities of cooperation, and desire to develop a practical form of cooperation (Smith, 1980, p. 78)

Although Smith then explains that most of the past agreements/projects were empty of meaning or value, it appears that the economic crises of the 1970s and the demand for practical action had suddenly pushed activity forward, though unevenly, and included the formation of trans-frontier institutions in Europe. One sign of this was a proliferation of cross-European acronyms of organizations created to provide a European-level forum for academics and administrators (Smith, 1980, p. 92):

> They are a 'genuine growth point for European cooperation' for specialist groups. A new start which is determined not by broad unitary goals or ambitious Europeaness but institutional reciprocity and a sense of practicality. (Smith, 1980, p. 93)

So, for example, in the field of higher education, by 1982, it was possible to observe that there was a wide variety of interested parties engaging in cooperation activities, including institutions:

> universities and non universities institutes of HE [higher education], together with sub units, the coordinating bodies and government education departments, ministries of foreign affairs and international organizations ... and individuals, through mobility projects, cooperation in teaching and research, exchange of ideas and information, use of research equipment and teaching aids, setting up European Centres of Higher Education and Research, and harmonization of courses. To enable these things to happen, a wide range of instruments were brought into play: multilateral and bilateral agreements, specific measures (subsidies, scholarships, recognition of

qualifications), regulations on legal status, information services, etc. (Leibrandt, 1982, p. 82)

Governing by Cooperation

Cooperation, an innocent word, designed to reassure Ministers from the Member States of the European Community that they could come together to consider common concerns in the educational field without fear of legal intervention or harmonizing initiatives from Community involvement that might be justified on the basis of the Treaty of Rome. (Fogg & Jones, 1985, p. 293)

They were far from the bold, open terms of the resolution adopted by the ministers of education less than three years earlier in November 1971, which advocated the 'definition of a European model of culture in correlation with European integration'. One of the reasons for this change in attitude was certainly the arrival in 1973 of three new Member States, two of which (Denmark and the United Kingdom) had a strong tradition of decentralisation.

It was this uneasiness which led the ministers of education to design a formula to advance collaboration which is unique within the machinery of the Community, for it combines the classical institutional machinery and procedures of the Council of the European Community with a voluntary commitment of the education ministers of the Nine to work together on a continuing basis outside the legal framework of the Council. (Jones, quoted in Pépin, 2006, p. 66)

Their arrival at the same time as Janne's report stalled action for some time:

it took almost three years of hard negotiations between the Commission and the national governments before the ground rules for educational cooperation could be agreed. These were designed with careful ambiguities, offering safeguards to reluctant Europeans yet confirming a degree of Community commitment to develop educational cooperation. (Jones, cited in Pépin, 2006, p. 68)

As Pépin (2006) argues:

This first action programme was both recapitulative and forward-looking. It was recapitulative because it covered the ideas voiced in the Spinelli and Janne reports and the most important positions (resolution of 1971, communication from the Commission of 1974 and resolution of 1974) on the subject

of mobility, language learning, cooperation in higher
education and a European dimension to education. (p. 69)

But education was future focused as well and the European dimension
had begun to materialize finally:

The action envisaged was based on much more than merely a
connection with the labour market. It focused on education as
a sphere in which to promote the notion of European unity
and as a fundamental element in the development of equal
opportunities (Pépin, 2006, p. 69)

A Community infrastructure for education had begun to be constructed:
there was an Education Committee connected to the Commission;
significant funding streams; developing relations with the employment
portfolio (and merger in 1981), and so with ministers of education and
employment. As the goals of the Community became more ambitious,
and focused on the economy:

the new emphasis on education as an instrument of both
economic and social policy is being pursued vigorously (Fogg
& Jones, 1985, p. 299)

The development of infrastructure, close relations and an emerging
agenda is important in the history of European education policy, but one
of the most distinctive, and influential, ideas of this period was
cooperation. Created through necessity, the concept of cooperation
appeared to be inclusive, welcoming and supportive, and worked at
different levels of the system. Apparently transparent, it had the
advantage of being 'a new form of controlling machinery to have
oversight' of the field (Fogg & Jones, 1985, p. 294). Involving
practitioners, professionals and social partners, it supported and
encouraged networking in various forms, and as this new sociality grew
thicker, mobilizing more actors across borders, Member States became
more enthusiastic as well; indeed working groups 'draw in officials from
practically every department of Ministries of Education, implicating
them directly in the Community experience' (Fogg & Jones, 1985, p. 298).
The Commission realized that

if cooperation was the fruit of necessity in the field of
education – since none of the traditional Community
instruments could be applied – cooperation was also a most
productive form of action equally applicable and quite as
relevant to other areas of Community policy, particularly in
social affairs and employment. (Fogg & Jones, 1985, p. 298)

The idea of cooperation as a governing approach, distinctively
educational, risked anarchy in action but faced the impossibility of top-
down approaches in this field. Education, although at the cusp of the

Community's broader agenda, was paving the way for integration, not only on the symbolic and discursive plane, but also through cooperation at a policy level, mobilizing networks, associations and a number of education players across Europe.

Culture and Affinity

A constant strand in the idea of the European dimension was the creation of a common identity, fabricated through cultural symbols and exchange, to produce affinity with Europe: 'a European model of culture correlating with European integration' (Comenius Action 1 – European Education Projects [EEPs], 1987 p. 11). Nation-states had treated identity formation as a key part of state formation; so, a similar process in the Community, binding an educational and cultural strategy, was described as an 'exceptional source of development, progress and culture (EEPs, 1987, p. 11). It would affirm a common space.

In 1971, the ministers of education, following the intentions of the Conference of Heads of State meeting at the Hague (in 1969), decided to create a working party which would devise a European Centre for the Development of Education (CEDEFOP), a way of financing it and a way to establish forms of active cooperation in the field of education. This step was preceded by reliance on the Council for Cultural Cooperation (within the Council of Europe), established in 1962. Again, in 1974, the ministers of education reaffirmed their new direction. They began their Resolution by repeating their mantra about Europe as an exceptional source of culture, by confirming that allowance must be made for the 'traditions of each country' and that education cannot be seen merely as 'a component of economic life' (EEPs, 1987, p. 15). An 'imagined community' of Europeans was coaxed into being by cross-institutional collaborations in education, especially around and through Socrates and Erasmus programmes. Increasingly, the place of culture is seen as protecting Europe against globalization. European identity meant having required knowledge and competences, recognizing membership of a common social and cultural area and developing mutual understanding within it. The dominant strand of identity is now more focused on individuated qualities, projected into a new space, than on a located citizen, inquiring into the places of others.

By 1976, the other aspect of this modernizing policy, of using education to create a new cultural identity, was being sustained by familiar projects on cross-institutional collaboration, documentation and statistics, recognition of qualifications and other aspects of a market in education, which are part of the continuing 'calculative rationality' of the modern state (Bauman, 1992). Cooperation in the field of education in Europe started as early as the 1970s with the first Community action programme (1975). The first 10 years of its implementation (1976-84) established the processes of the collaboration through transnational pilot projects, study visits and exchanges of information and experience. These developments:

> engendered a form of cooperation within the Community
> framework, which, in a way, was the first application of the
> principle of subsidiarity before it was defined and the first
> demonstration that it was possible, in a Community that was
> on the path to integration, to cooperate in areas that were
> fundamental to the structure of the nation states while fully
> respecting the diversity of national situations and the powers
> of Member States. (Pépin, 2006, p. 25)

In 1983 the European Community heads of government signed the 'Solemn Declaration on European Union' in Stuttgart, inviting member states 'to promote European awareness and to undertake joint action in various cultural areas' – these were information, education, audio-visual policy and the arts (European Council, 1983). A year later, through the 'Television without Frontiers' directive, it was suggested that 'European unification will only be achieved if Europeans want it. Europeans will only want it if there is such a thing as European identity' (European Council, 1984a). Since there was no legal basis for a specific cultural policy, a number of ad hoc 'cultural actions' were justified for their economic pertinence in the expanding field of the culture industry (Forrest, 1993). The most significant development of the 1980s was the European Council's decision to create an ad hoc 'Committee for a People's Europe', chaired by the Italian Member of the European Parliament (MEP) Pietro Adonnino. The Committee produced two influential reports, as part of the project of building Europe: two of their recommendations included strengthening the European cultural sector and providing reciprocal recognition of equivalent diplomas and professional qualifications (Shore, 2000). According to the reports, 'through action in the areas of culture and communication, which are essential to the European identity and the Community's image in the minds of its people, support for the advancement of Europe can and must be sought' (Adonnino, 1985, p. 21). There were suggestions for the foundation of a European Academy of Science, European sports teams, school exchange programmes, voluntary work camps for young people, and, in general, the introduction of a stronger European dimension in education, including 'the preparation and availability of appropriate school books and teaching materials' (Adonnino, 1985, p. 24). The introduction of the European flag of the 12 yellow stars against the blue background became the key symbol in European consciousness-raising:

> Twelve was a symbol of perfection and plenitude, associated
> equally with the apostles, the sons of Jacob, the tables of the
> Roman legislator, the labours of Hercules, the hours of the day,

the months of the year, or the signs of the Zodiac. Lastly, the circular layout denoted union. (Council of Europe, quoted in Shore, 2000, p. 47)

The era of the 'Euro-symbols' had begun: the Community funded the formation of an 'EC Youth Orchestra'; an 'Opera Centre'; the conservation of the Parthenon and monasteries in Mount Athos; the 'European Literature Prize'; the 'European Woman of the Year' award; the 'Jean Monnet Awards'; the cultural capitals of Europe; the 'European Year of the Cinema'; the 'European Year of the Environment' and so on (Shore, 2000). Far from transcending the hegemony of the nation-state ideology, the new Europe was being constructed with the tools of what Shore calls a 'conservative current of nineteenth-century social evolutionist thought' (2000, p. 50). Nairn describes the process of the building of the European identity, not as the end of the nation-state, but as the creation of a 'super-nation-state founded on European chauvinism' (Nairn, 1977, p. 16). Retrospectively, it is interesting to note that at the beginning of the 1990s Europe's constructed 'Other' was not illegal immigrants, but the wave of Americanization dominating Europe from the west. *Le défi americain* repeatedly appears in Commission discourse and other official documentation as threatening the European common cultural heritage, which, although it had deep roots in the history of the European peoples, the Commission still needed to 'defend' against and raise 'awareness' of (Shore, 2000).

At the beginning of the 1990s, the collapse of communism in Eastern Europe and the outlook of German reunification had already led to a commitment to reinforce the Community's international position through the Treaty on European Union (TEU), signed on 7 February 1992 and in operation from 1 November 1993. Known as the Maastricht Treaty, it was to become a landmark in the history of European integration as the culmination of the 'Single European Act' of 1985 which established the objective of the common market. In addition, after more than 15 years of activity, the fields of education and culture were acquiring a clear legal basis within the EU policy framework. The Maastricht Treaty was the pinnacle of a series of symbolic decisions taken at Community level in the 1980s, such as the issuing of a single European passport, the abolishing of all police and customs formalities for people crossing intra-Community borders, as well as the considerations for the creation of a single flag, a European anthem, European sports teams and the creation of European coinage, namely the ECU (European Council, 1984b).

Above all, the Treaty on the European Union was the first time that education and culture was being acknowledged as an inherent part of the integration process. Vocational training was slightly weakened in the new arrangement, since it lost its unique standing and became part of the wider framework in the cooperation in education, culture and social work. Although the process had already started in the 1980s, these were the first firm steps in the shift from the 'technocrats' Europe' to a 'Europe of the peoples'. Although Articles 126 and 127 of the Maastricht Treaty (1992) declared that there would be no harmonization of European education systems nor that a common European education model would be promoted, fields of activity such as language learning, youth exchanges, collaboration amongst educational institutions and especially student and teacher mobility were to receive far greater economic sustenance and policy significance as the 'complementary' competences of the European Union. Maastricht signalled the vital ingredient that had been missing from the recipe so far: legitimacy for the European cause. If there was a need for a Commission, a Parliament, a Council, a Court of Justice and a Central Bank, surely there was a need to create a European *demos,* a transnational European public whose interests the Union would represent.

Indeed, at the beginning of the 1990s the Union seemed to undergo a deep crisis: its elite administration with its bureaucratic and centralized character did not appear alluring any more. Once again, Europe needed a unifying myth. The common agricultural or competition policy did not appear sufficient to justify the European project; education would have to become the vital ingredient in building the 'people's Europe', in order to 'make people more aware of their European identity in anticipation of the creation of a European cultural area' (Council of the European Communities, 1987, p. 37). 'Europeanization' found in the fields of education and culture some of the most influential carriers of a common European consciousness; that is, all those factors, abstract and concrete, formal and informal, individual and collective, which have been slowly changing the ways Europe is represented. These have not only been the official and unofficial representations fostered by the Union or by the Member States themselves. The Erasmus programme, for instance, although already significantly successful by 1992, was to increase the numbers of student exchanges across Europe during the 1990s to hundreds of thousands. Europe was not just a myth, but a reality for the educational experiences and exchanges of thousands of Europeans.

By the late 1990s, the two new education programmes, 'Socrates' and 'Leonardo', with significant amounts of funding (933 million ECU for Socrates and 794 million ECU for Leonardo), were formed. They both ran from 1995 to 1999. Socrates had the objective 'to contribute to the development of quality education and training and the creation of an open European area for cooperation in education' and in particular to 'develop the European dimension in education in order to promote citizenship' (Pépin, 2006, p. 170). It followed three strands: Higher Education (Erasmus), School Education (Comenius) and Language Learning (Lingua). The instruments of cooperation, according to the programme, would be institutional contracts, transnational projects, mobility and networks. 'Leonardo' aimed at implementing a Community vocational training programme, signalling the increasing significance given to the development of lifelong learning in the knowledge society. Both programmes were continued for a second phase (2000-2006) and are now replaced by the new Commission's Lifelong Learning programme – the first time that, rather than a scholarly name, a more 'pragmatic' name has been given to a European education programme.

However, as with the old empires, the arrival of success for the Union had perhaps already sown the seeds of a crisis. Due to enlargement and globalization, debates were soon to change the focus of the integration process from uniting the peoples of Europe under a common destiny, to finding urgent and joint responses to new challenges. According to Pépin:

> It was now more necessary than ever to create this 'ever closer union among the people of Europe' which had been asserted since the beginning by successive treaties and could not be achieved by economic integration alone. The globalisation of trade and the information and communication technologies had an ever greater impact on how and where knowledge was transferred, education and training systems being at the top of the list. (2006, p. 156)

Indeed, as early as 1994, the EU White Paper on growth, competitiveness and employment supported the need to take action in the field of lifelong learning. In 1995 the White Paper 'Teaching and Learning –towards the learning society' had already begun constructing the Europe of the future. Europe's culture and civilization appeared of less significance in this new official discourse: 'Tomorrow's society will be a society which invests in knowledge, a society of teaching and learning, in which each individual will build up his or her own qualifications. In other words, a learning society' (European Commission, 1996). By the late 1990s, this familiar strategy, a shadow of the past of the main partners, had evolved into a different identity altogether. Affinity to Europe based on cross-cultural access, and situated within nation-states and official identities, had moved to another kind of imagined Europe in which innovation, research, education and training were its pillars. This 'imagined community' had radically altered dimensions: it was a community like a major corporation was a community, and not a community in the older languages of culture, nation or region.

A European collaboration based on cultural transfer and exchange (*circa* the 1970s) has been replaced by 'European cooperation networks' pooling European excellence and creating real European expertise. This new community would not have to be an imagined one, based on the interweaving of education programmes, cultural symbols and notions of common identity. It would be constructed by harmonizing system elements, especially qualifications; mutually recognizing them; and building interoperable standards which would create working webs and networks, the accumulating basis for a common system of education.

From Chaotic Uniformity to Networked Cooperation

The gradual working out of underlying European dimension ideas within projects and initiatives reveals how the Europeanizing policy discourse and its instruments became interlinked and bound together across new programmes and enterprises in the 1990s. This process was fraught with political dangers, even when ministers were in agreement, and the Commission did not have sufficient funding or its own expert managers. However, new programme documents, even apparently out of range of education, appeared to be composite constructions in which older ideas and projects are rewoven and revitalized by attaching themselves to technology-based infrastructure and economy-focused projects. Applicants had to use and re-use key established policy referents.

As new funded projects developed, they could become active and not passive agents of policy, especially when operating in funding models which depended on constant applications for organizational stability. Projects metamorphosed into immutable elements in networks and policy areas. An interesting example of the way in which Europeanizing processes could emerge attached to new technologies and older policy trends, and then mutate into recognizable but active autonomous sites of Europeanization is the foundation and growth of the European Schoolnet. In 2009, the Schoolnet was described as:

> a key success story at international level as a network of 31 Ministries of Education in Europe and beyond. It was created more than 10 years ago to encourage innovation in teaching and learning, supported through the use of Information and Communications Technologies (ICT). Its key stakeholders are Ministries of Education, schools, teachers and researchers ... At pan-EU level, European Schoolnet is the only organisation with such a mandate and was one of the first school networks across the globe ... Its activities are divided into three strands (1) Policy, research and innovation, (2) Schools services, and (3) Learning resource exchange and interoperability of digital content. All the activities involve networking with a wide variety of actors in education and their supporting administration systems, i.e. policy-makers, technical experts, individual teachers, pupils and researchers who are active in the field. (Scimeca, 2009, p. 475)

The ideas which permeated the Schoolnet can be traced back to 1978 when the Commission promoted the 'European dimension' in *Educational Activities with a European Content: the study of the European Community in Schools* and 1988 when the ministers created a new resolution about Community education policy. The idea of a European dimension was mainly concerned with the school curriculum across the school years and institutions; creative seminars to conceptualize and develop it were planned; school-to-school relations, twinning between schools, were to be encouraged; an annual Europe Day was to be produced. By 1992, the year of the Maastricht Treaty, the idea of a European dimension had begun to focus much more on the mobility of students and teachers across Europe; the recognition of national diplomas; cooperation between education institutions and the rise of data about the education systems of the Member States. The 1996 White Paper on the Learning Society (European Commission, 1996) transformed the thinking again by linking the use of technology and the creation of new European education software to the idea of the Information Society. The idea of a European dimension in education had gradually shifted away from being a sensitive political issue, working across state borders, and become embedded in a common economic and commercial policy which placed the European education 'sector' within a European economic trading zone. Old political sensitivities about political demarcations in a stable world had crumbled with the risks of uncertainty and the recognition that Europe was the only way forward for all. The idea of education, a state responsibility under subsidiarity, had metamorphosed into learning. This shift moved it politically from the responsibility of ministers of education and into a restructured overall economic goal across the states and their government departments. It had two broad aims and an overall strategy; the first:

> focuses on the need for a broad knowledge base and the second is designed to build up abilities for employment and economic life. Establishing the learning society will also depend on how those involved and the institutions in education and training pursue the developments already under way in the Member States. (European Commission, 1996, p. 5)

The Education dimension had moved from the purview of education and out across the Commission, and in doing so, it was seen, as learning, as the way to manage new skills and radical shifts in society, and as the site of a major change in pedagogy and resources. It was now viewed as a hybrid private/public arena, as it would be both an opportunity for European technology and software companies and impossible without them. In 1995 a powerful task force on education multimedia software, with about 50 million euros of funding, was set up and over the next few years, it fostered a number of key European programmes to speed up the growth of information and communication technologies, and a large number of multimultimedia projects were selected for support. A specific action plan, 'Learning in the Information Society', was launched in 1996 to support the introduction of a programme for communication between schools.

A sign of the political, economic and educational significance of the mid 1990s was the fact that change was being promoted by new accession countries, like Sweden. The Swedish Minister of Education, Yva Johansson, launched a European Schoolnet initiative in December 1996, took it to an informal meeting of the Council in Amsterdam on March 1997 and received support: 'the importance of this project ... is confirmed by the strong support it has immediately received by all Member States' (Letter from Cresson, 2 April 1997).

The Schoolnet was to be funded through applications to Community programmes and immediately had to produce a major application to the action plan, 'Learning in the Information Society', even though it was clearly seen as a powerful Member States initiative. The Swedish government supported it financially during this period. The application had to manage two separate groups in software and education, many of whom were new to each other, in designing a platform and a framework of activity. It would be a new kind of network, built upon a stable software platform:

> [it] aims at establishing a network of networks for the delivery via the internet of tools and pedagogical information services with a European added-value to schools in Europe and for the common development and exchange of information as regards the use of ICT in schools. ... to develop and set up a model platform offering pupils and teachers access to high quality information and services of European interest; develop and validate multimedia tools; establish a network of 500 innovative schools (Thematic Network in Teacher Education Archive, Umeå, unpublished proposal)

Proposed sub-projects included classroom library services and a virtual teachers' college alongside web platform standards and open standard tools for the multimedia lab. Original planning for the European Virtual Teachers' College came from a partner, the Thematic Network for Teacher Education in Europe, funded by the Commission, and included ideas for virtual lecture halls, notice boards, conferencing groups, handbooks and specialist resources:

> a specialist site or space in which all teacher education takes place, just like a very advanced university or regional site including special guest speakers; courses and modules – joint development and joint cooperation within the field of IT

[across Europe]. (Kallos letter, May 1997, in Thematic Network in Teacher Education Archive, Umeå)

The Schoolnet's final and successful application is interesting at several levels. Its discourse mixes up the immediate past, present needs and future possibilities in European education. In effect, it promised to deliver that which had escaped the Commission and the ministers in the past, an effective and ambitious but virtual European education system or area. Following the 1980s and early 1990s, it continues the reference to the European dimension: it aims to be a site of good practice in curricula and the training of teachers, develop school twinning and European Netdays. It would operate in the preferred European way of governance: through public and private partnerships, cooperation, and as a network of networks. It would have European added value, produce transnational and pan-European cooperation. Reflecting new EU priorities, it would develop a common platform for education in Europe, with common standards in learning software, and the development of educational multimedia resources (using Europe's audiovisual and publishing sectors as stakeholders. In effect, it would stitch together for the future 'an open European information network infrastructure' for education.

Within a few years, Schoolnet had become a vehicle for drawing together the disparate groups needed to deliver the new learning infrastructure:

> policy makers, pedagogical and technological researchers,
> innovative teachers and school managers, school network
> operators, infrastructure suppliers, commercial hardware and
> tools' vendors, content developers and publishers, standards
> bodies, partners active in projects related to wireless
> networking and mobile learning, home networking and 'smart
> homes'. (European Schoolnet, 2002a, pp. 3/4)

It had become more than a network of networks though; now it is a European policy actor and enabler itself. Its original tasks, 'training for teachers in the use of ICT' (Pépin, 2006 p. 432) and 'raising awareness of the potential of new technologies' (p. 433), had revealed the problems in this area: 'an increasing commitment to the introduction of ICT by governments and the education system are failing to demonstrate progress, success, and the added value of new learning methods' (European Schoolnet, 2002a, p. 24). Its solution to this drew it closer to the new EU aims around lifelong learning, as it wished to go beyond 'formal educational institutions' and could operate in the home and the community with new technologies (European Schoolnet, 2002a, pp. 3/4). Schoolnet is able to argue for an EU policy which is barely in place, 'eLearning', and intends to produce future policy scenarios, identify innovation inhibitors in the system and provide policy roadmaps for change (European Schoolnet, 2002b). It continues to combine leading-edge thinking in the learning/technology interface; indeed it represents a new hybrid form, and its thinking goes beyond the previous decades' thinking of schools as national, bordered assets which have to be cautiously encouraged and moves swiftly into the problems of European 'schools as learning organizations' and the need to produce 'agents of organizational change'. Schools are not to be viewed as users of ICT but as commercial test beds, markets and as production sites of technology integration:

> technical integration can be achieved involving broadband
> delivery, wireless networking, access via new varieties of
> mobile/handheld devices, new types of knowledge mapping,
> more intuitive interfaces etc. (European Schoolnet, 2002a,
> pp. 3/4)

At the same time, Schoolnet combines European schools together into a virtual education system or a series of 'online educational communities' where thousands of teachers and pupils collaborate together across borders, for which it provides platforms and tools. Mainly secondary teachers in 30 countries used their communities to develop curriculum-based teaching and extracurricular teaching activities.

Through this interesting and creative institution, the weakness of the past has been overcome. The old EU politics of defensive ministries and subsidiarity have been bypassed, the conservative public sector of education has been breached and the private sector has penetrated education as a market and a site of production.

At the same time, networks could mobilize, enfold and enable new actors, including teachers, and if stable and successful, push Europeanizing processes wider and faster across different European scales and sites. If networks can remain pertinent and stable then they breed actors and nodes, and the development of significant platforms was a key element in this process. The networks, their work and communications and the platform constituted a 'home'. A home is a complex idea, involving social, cultural and work elements, associated with family and community, and most of all, with identity. The new European teacher began to have homes which were not local, bounded or merely regional and national, they were also of a new European form.

CHAPTER 4

Governing Education: the use of persuasive and unobtrusive power in the EU

Introduction

Governing acts in Europe are complex but one of the consistent ways of managing the construction of the European Union is the way a field is mobilized and persuaded into existence; this is particularly apparent in the field of education and training. The European Policy Space in Education is more than an ill-defined space of regulation or activity; it is a space of attraction and meaning, in which soft power is at work, creating a space to which actors are drawn (Nye, 2004). So, the space is produced and re-produced. The lack of visibility of this strengthening policy space and its changing significance and definition has meant that a range of particular governing devices (networking, seminars, reviews, expert groups, etc.), described here as 'soft governance', have not been examined as a force in the Europeanization of education (Ahonen, 2001; Lawn, 2006). The idea of soft power is viewed here as the cultivation of support and the creation of meaning inside and around the idea of a European Union, and its relation to the field of education in particular.

Using these ideas, the focus of this chapter is on the way that an association came into being in the final decade of the last century, at a time when European education policy, and its benchmarking, was beginning to expand. As the policy space in education is being created, from within, by policy actors of various kinds operating in and across the new organizations, the role of associations in constructing this area is important. The association, the European Educational Research Association, grew with the policy space of education but it found it difficult to create a platform, that is a viewpoint and communication infrastructure, and even maintain stability in a situation which was both new and demanding. The European Commission has always had an interest in the stakeholders, social partners and associations working in education; it wanted close cooperation with them, developed contacts and exchanges, and practised an 'open door policy' according to Pépin (2006, p. 86). Over time, European associations were created and accepted as partners; for example, the CRE (European Rectors' Conference) in 1959; the ETUCE (the European Trade Union Committee for Education) in 1975; the ATEE (Association for Teacher Education in Europe) in 1976; the ESHA (European School Heads Association) in 1988; and the EAEA (European Association for the Education of Adults) in 1999. This approval was important, as the next step was being accepted as a funded partner:

> Many European-scale projects supported by the Commission came from these organisations. The development of the Socrates programme in the 1990s contributed towards reinforcing the participation of unions and associations in pan-European education projects. This programme also allowed for the regular consultation of the social partners and associations involved in the field of education at European level. (Pépin, 2006, p. 86)

Actors of many kinds are drawn into the European policy space, and as the EU developed, many European associations came into existence to represent their subjects or interests. Through the work of one association, the European Educational Research Association (EERA), we can explore the problems of acting as a 'partner' within a new policy space coming into being. At the same time that EERA began to form itself, and its members learnt to work across borders, the European policy space they worked within became more defined, active, performance based and most of all, governed. Studies of EERA show its enormous difficulties in entering 'Europe' as a social and knowledge partner, and the problems that an EU, viewed here as the Commission, has in governing through unstable and voluntaristic loose associations. Associations and networks operate laterally and horizontally across borders, within a spectrum of relations, and are based upon trust and fair exchange. They work with the flow of communications and data in Europe, are effective in small-scale activity and retain strong cultural strength among members even after network collapse. The mobilizing and communicative energy in European networks is important to the achievement of new European objectives. Using the idea of platform, we look at the foundation of one European association as it attempted to engage with this new European policy arena, and then examine the way in which soft governance, as a European method of governance, attracts and supports associations and networks, as it ties them into its programmes and work. It fosters their pursuit of meaning.

Governing Associations Softly

The governing context in which the association, EERA, had to work was constituted by several features; these were an emphasis on networks, on partners, on expert actors and practitioners, and on meaning. As EERA came into being, it had to face its organizational problems but, even more critically, the invitation to act within and produce a European space for education (and research).

A key element is the range of networking which is taking place within the field of education, partly supported by the Commission, with features including simple informational activities extending to complex, research-based inquiry; interest-driven pressure, professional or research groups; and public or private organization entrepreneurial activity. Castells described networks as:

> made of many cultures, many values, many projects, that cross
> through the minds, and inform the strategies of the various
> participants in the networks, changing them at the same pace
> as the network's members, and following the organizational
> and cultural transformations of the units of the network. It is a
> culture, indeed, but a culture of the ephemeral, a culture of
> each strategic decision, a patchwork of experiences and
> interests. (1996, p. 198)

Within this field of activity, the soft tool of networking is significant. It has within it always, the potential associated with markets, private and public partnerships and the new ways of supporting public activity, to be crucial for governing, but a governing which attracts as much as it disciplines. In the field of education in particular, the governing of education in Europe relies upon a range of old and new public, semi-public, and private actors for its emergence. This Europeanization of education 'space' can be examined through a linking of social structures, networks and actors at the local, national and European levels and, in turn, may reveal the formation of new European identities within emergent policy networks. There is an increasing complexity of governance, involving a range of partners from state and civil society, in informal and interdependent relations, exchanging resources and knowledge cooperatively. The European Union has itself been characterized as a 'network of networks' (Leonard, 1998, p. 7).

The governance of Europe has specific problems and forms. To create and manage policy, a range of partners, at different levels of government, has to be negotiated with; they exist within complex networks, which span intergovernmental, producer, professional and expert forms (Bellier & Wilson, 2000; Shore, 2000). They may represent highly organized industry or voluntary sector groups or loose, but important, specialist academic associations. Increasingly, it appears that these networks, woven into sets of linked relations, represent a form of governance unique in Europe, crossing state boundaries, old government divisions and traditions of work and administration. The informality of their organization, the complexity of their knowledge relations and exchanges, the hybridity of their institutional association combine with their overall interdependence to produce a distinctive form of governance in Europe. This form of governance in education cannot be understood as simply instrumental in transmitting policy or in mediating it. EU governance has become associated with the management of key spaces: regions, cities, networks, borders. So, the European Educational Research Association was created at a time when 'education' appeared as an area of policy under the Maastricht Treaty and when networks were a useful tool in the Europeanizing process. Networks weren't just useful as conduits of policy or ideas, but as mobilizing agents for policy. The construction of Europe was taking place through the cultivation of support and the creation of meaning, just as much as by trade, regulation, soft law or cross-border agreement. A key element has been the production of an attractive idea; the ambiguous, modernizing and mobilizing idea of a project, and a concomitant 'space' to be created (Laïdi, 1998). It is a mobilizing, soft governance which its subjects may be attracted to because of the attempt to nurture support and meaning about it from them. It is a soft governance in which pedagogy, learning and education have come to represent a governing arena. A space may be opened up that can be occupied by actors who find opportunities to create new meanings; in Laïdi's view, these spaces of meaning are symbolic spaces which transcend national spaces and which strive to produce a 'regional imaginary' (Laïdi, 2003, p. 2). Meaning creates affinity. and the deliberate involvement of the Association in Commission meetings with an opportunity to shape policy was attractive. Affinity is created in the education arena through the professional space it offers across Europe, which associations and actors have used to generate new spaces for action and meaning (Lawn, 2001a). Similarly, networks have been funded to stitch together new actors into communities of interest, working across a range of subjects, and gradually coalescing under the colours of lifelong learning.

Non-territorial, horizontal networks, involving actors drawn from outside governmental organizations, are visibly at work, creating a space around their interests and trying to overcome problems of legitimacy. They appear to be self-governing networks of actors mobilizing capacities for action, appearing autonomous yet often relying, at some level, on governmental power. Increasingly, it appears that networks, woven into sets of linked relations, represent a common form of governance in Europe, crossing national boundaries, old government divisions and traditions of work and administration. Network governance operates within a rich matrix of flows and scapes, and on different scales, involving actors pulled in through partnerships, associated initiatives, professional innovations and manager networking, all connected by funding searches, performance improvement and interest.

In effect, academics and experts, often through their associations or specialist groupings, act as new political actors. Professional associations are becoming crucial in the governance of many areas of EU policy, especially ICT (Knill, 2001) where they act to provide expertise in areas where the Commission is weak, and where intervention involves a range of heterogeneous actors. Associations have begun to alter their structures, from federalist and national, to European and individual membership, to cope with the new demands upon them in providing expertise, acting as policy mediators between the national and the transnational, and supporting ambitious European goals. Even education is not immune from this as European-wide associations struggle to achieve for their members information and influence, and cope with Commission expectations about their stability and expertise. Experts work with an expertise which is portable. They act as points of distribution for the ideas of Europeanization, creating, imagining and transmitting, and existing within and outwith diverse steered partnerships.

This European education space is not an overall description of a known topography, containing fixed and identified elements, but instead, it describes a place coming into being, which has been catalyzed into creation through a mode of ordering (Law, 1994), provided by political necessity, commercial demand and professional obligation, and structured by new technologies and virtual presences. This governance sphere exists in the same space, the same networks and even within the same communications as the knowledge-producing relations of networking in education. It may not be entirely homologous with it but there is a close fit between the ordering of this space and the activities of associations and networks, and individual actors. It operates in a dynamic market, where its usefulness is validated in the different contexts, where diverse forms of specialized knowledge are needed. Socially distributed knowledge has fluid forms of production: it is produced in an array of sites, often linked together, across private and public organizations, with a range of skill levels and applications. It drives forward the formation of a policy space, by circulating ideas, promoting the capacity of individuals to generate and process information, and of networks to realize its value.

Associations and Networks

We want to look in more detail at the difficulties that the newly formed EERA has had in understanding its situation in Europe, making sense of it and acting within Europe as a 'partner' and developing a platform, a space of meaning for its members.

The formation of a national educational research association in itself is not an unusual thing; the American Educational Research Association was founded in 1916, several of the European associations were the product of the expansion of education in the late 1960s [2] and the Australian Association for Research in Education was founded in 1974. The European Educational Research Association finally came together in 1994, formed from a growing partnership between national associations in an ever-forming Europe. One of the features national associations have in common is a sense of the national system and bounded territory in which they work, and their emergence as a critical mass of researchers. Their foundation question assumed that they worked in a known place with familiar features, and was not the most common European association question, 'where are we?' National educational researchers did not begin by trying to 'name the parts' of their educational landscape so much as by clarifying how a reasonably clear and known landscape was to be studied. Association members would work in proximity or at a distance from power but they were unlikely to feel dislocated or disoriented. One way or another, they knew where they were.

On the other hand, EERA's foundation question *really* was 'where are we'? The tensions caused in a voluntary, professional association, constructing itself from different associations with diverse histories and practices, and trying to work within a rapidly changing European policy space in education and research, were at the heart of its problems. The concept of a networked governance in the European Union implicated the EERA, along with other European associations, in knowledge and power questions which it had to understand and handle. Early ideas of a 'band of brothers and sisters' in a new European accord of their own making, a cross-border collegiality, have been overtaken by shifts in the definition and governance of the space they have entered. Fraternal and sisterly links and collaborative practices, crucial to the formation of the Association, have not been sufficient as the European policy space they work within has become more defined, active, performance based and most of all, governed.

The tendency in European political studies to emphasize the forms of integration and adaptation in which administrative, regulatory and professional development systems are gradually woven together has obscured a less developed cultural analysis, which emphasizes the processes of production and consumption of policy. Europe is imagined as a 'community of ourselves' in EU policy documents, and a cultural policy analysis frame throws into relief its sharing of meanings, the production of identity and its emerging commonalities. Space is reconfigured constantly as the new policy spaces – city-to-city networks, peripheral countries, horizontal networks, central and border regions and other sites – work with each other via a web of distributed policy making in multiple centres.

The Association, viewed as a network, may be a useful analytical tool for understanding the form of European governance; mapping its development is critical to an understanding of changing educational governance. It is possible to view networks, woven into sets of linked relations, as representing a form of governance and to test them by analysing ways in which they are both constructing and being constructed by a new kind of policy space (Eising & Kohler-Koch, 1999).

The ideas of network governance, in opposition to markets and hierarchies, fit the European Union very well. To maximize the governing of the large number of states within it, and to manage the sensitivities of the national legislatures and agencies, the EU has a number of strategies, which include regulatory mechanisms, performance indicators, transnational agreements and network coordination and support. Networks work with the flow of communications and data in Europe, are effective in small-scale activity and retain strong cultural strength among members even after network collapse. The mobilizing and communicative energy in European networks is important to the achievement of new European objectives, and the activity of the Directorates-General in the Commission has been consistently directed at social partnership and associational modes of governing. Non-commercial associations, with a voluntary membership, working in national systems of rapid change, and struggling to enter into a new form of cross-national association, found themselves in a policy space which demanded more of them. Incentives, support and 'modernization' were on offer, yet each step of engagement led to significant efforts of mobilization and was succeeded by disappointment or renewed efforts. The gap between the demands upon them and their practical situation was often too great.

Experts and Associations – EERA

The first European Conference on Educational Research (ECER) took place on 22-25 June 1992, two years before the foundation of the EERA in Strasbourg in 1994. The ECER took place at the University of Twente through the initiative of Dutch education researchers, especially Professor Tjeerd Plomp. It had been proposed that the tenth annual conference of the Dutch association, the VOR (Vereniging voor Onderwijs Research) should, in the year of the signing of the EU Maastricht Treaty (which included education formally for the first time in an EU Treaty), be a European conference as well as a national one. The ECER 1992 letter of invitation, sent out widely across Europe, mentions the creation of the Single European Act (which now included education policy) and that a 'new educational policy is emerging in Europe' and educational research needs to 'broaden its perspective'. At the time there were few comparative studies on European educational research, and educational research was included in the 'Targeted Socio-Economic Research' (TSER) programme, initiated in 1994, for the first time. It was an opportune time to create a European association. Additional funding to support the ECER was found when the European Commission was approached to support the Conference and instead of a direct grant, offered to pay for a feasibility study on the state of educational research in Europe. The study was focused on the question: 'Whether and under what conditions educational researchers from the member (and also other European) countries can be brought together' (Plomp, 1991, p. 1).

Plomp prepared a report for the European Community Task Force on Education, which evaluated the idea of a European educational research association and its different possible structures. Twenty-five researchers, a panel of experts, were consulted; they were drawn by Plomp from his contacts in the IEA of which he was Chair, and an appendix of national and European research associations and contacts was added. The report proposed a European Community Bureau to support researchers and their associations and as a platform to approach researchers on behalf of the Commission. The ECER 1992 was intended to represent some of the proposals in the report, such as starting to form a European association and creating a 'market for research' (showing national associations and their work).

Plomp had issued a special invitation to approximately 20 educational researchers to attend an informal meeting during the ECER 1992 to discuss the merits and desirability of setting up a European association in the field of educational research. This meeting was attended by 21 people from 10 countries (Belgium, England, Italy, Netherlands, Portugal, Scotland, Switzerland, Spain, Czech Republic and Hungary); some were representatives of national educational research organizations, while others were affiliated to a specialized association active in the area of educational research (Consortium of Higher Education Research [CHER], Consortium of Institutions for Development and Research in Education in Europe [CIDREE], European Association for Institutional Research [EAIR], European Association for Learning and Instruction [EARLI], International Congress for School Effectiveness and Improvement [ICSEI]). The meeting discussed the fact that the organization of educational research was still inadequate in several European countries, and, moreover, that international associations specializing in sub-areas of educational research did not seem to be willing to join an umbrella organization spanning the entire discipline; and they encouraged the European Commission to set up a Bureau of Education Research (Plomp, 1992). Apparently, there was a difference of opinion between the national and the specialized associations about the value of having a European educational research association. The meeting decided to establish 'an association of national associations of educational researchers', which would work with existing international associations – like EARLI, which would assist countries with 'weak or no infrastructure', and which would not replace national conferences. Eight national representatives met again at the ECER and intended to meet early in 1993 in Switzerland; they were from the United Kingdom, Sweden, Spain, Portugal, Italy, Hungary, the Czech Republic and the Netherlands. This second meeting of 'Representatives of National Associations for Research in Education in European Countries' decided to form a European educational research association quickly for several reasons: that strong associations should help the weak through exchange and transfer; that Europe was moving from uncoordinated to coherent activity in research; there was a need for an umbrella organization rather than specialized or area-specific associations; the Council of Europe and the OECD asked for a single organization across the whole of education research; and Eastern Europe needed to be brought into the fold (Gretler, 1994b).

The key discussions were on the relation between EERA and other associations and agencies, and the internal question of membership categories. At the time, EERA was conceived of as an 'umbrella' organization, an overarching and facilitating body, with membership drawn from specialized associations and from intergovernmental organizations (European Community, the Council of Europe, the OECD and UNESCO). If they were not to become members of this 'umbrella' organization, then EERA would have an obligation to cooperate and communicate with them. Institutes and individuals would become EERA members if they were members of their national or a specialized association. Another category, individual members, was created to allow individuals in countries without national associations to join, and was later widened to include countries that did have national associations.

The first Executive Committee met in Strasbourg in June 1994 and in essence, it had to decide on every aspect of the new Association immediately: it discussed its legal status, the roles of its Executive Members; an EERA Secretariat; a proposed EERA Newsletter; the offer from a publisher that EERA adopt their journal in educational research; the Call for Papers for the next year's Conference; and the structure of EERA's divisions or Special Interest Groups. It was decided to become a charity although the Committee also considered returning to the other options (limited company and European Interest Group). They began to compile a list of European associations and institutes of educational research and to write to them formally inviting them to join; they expected that some associations would become formal Special Interest Groups in EERA.

Since 1994 EERA, the aim of which is to include all national educational research associations in Europe, has grown steadily. EERA represented several associations but then began to act, in line with its aims, to mobilize others into existence, and some national associations came into existence in order to join EERA. In effect, it formed the main networking for the new policy space in education research. Soon, EERA was to adopt new regulations which allowed its Council to expand to include representatives from recognized educational research associations in every European country. Very soon, EERA members began to feel thwarted by the gap between the organic growth of professional and focused networking, which it represented, and, overall, the low-quality support infrastructure across Europe, which was impeding a constructive contribution to this crucial policy area, the 'European Space of Educational Research'.

Building a Platform: fluidity and stability in EERA

The Association and its Office were seen by Plomp as providing a 'platform and a vehicle' (Plomp, 1991, p. 10) for educational researchers in Europe to give 'voice'. In contemporary thinking, the idea of the platform merges two once separate forms, the place from which to speak, and the technology which enables communication. In a term like 'ideas platform', these two aspects are bound together and probably will be for some time. Also, the platform combines hardware and software, for example, an operating system, user interface, applications, and computers. In the mid 90s the idea of a platform was used metaphorically as a place in which discussions and exchanges could take place; this could be a room, a conference or a newsletter. It assumed a place for necessary democratic and expert exchanges. In its earlier mid 90s version and its contemporary one, a platform could involve a range of objects and texts, an array of bodies and cultures, and some form of ordering embedded in the event which binds people and meaning together. From its earliest days then, EERA conceived of its task as ordering and choreographing its members through the work of its Office. It implicitly and explicitly felt that it represented in this task the expression of European ideas, skills and interests in educational research, through interest and expert based exchanges. The work of EERA's Office, the symbol of EERA, and its 'home', was to represent, order and develop the new association or networking of European education researchers.

From the beginning, there were several problems to determine and analyse. The first was how to fund and organize an office when it was not clear what the extent and complexity of its tasks would be, and how they could be funded. The second reflected this imminent task in an uncertain situation – what did it mean to be a 'European' association and what were its obligations and precedents? Nearly every element of its situation was new or ambiguous and very few assumptions for action could be rendered solid; all appeared mutable. At an early conference in Lille, its new Secretary General spoke about its context:

> For academics in education, networks have begun to appear that are distinguishable from their older, national professional forms of association. One source, particular to Europe, is the range of supported networking which reflects the new governance of Europe (regions, transnational programmes, EU Declarations, etc.) and related funding (through Socrates, Thematic Networks, EU based research projects, etc.). Supported (partially funded) networks are a reflection of EU governance, and the close meshing of national governmental policies and programmes with European initiatives. These networks are expected to bind together individuals and institutions across Europe and to deliver products, either continuing relations with each other or through useful commodities. Other European features include new cross-university agreements and alliances supporting mobility of students and staff and joint production of education courses; education publishing (journals, books, etc.) across European markets; creation of cross-Europe 'pressure group' associationism (for example, a European association for special education or adult education) which can be treated as social partners by the EU. This new networking is underpinned by a new commerce of education and by the necessary information technologies which allow academics to manage communications and information flow easier than in the past. (Lawn, 2001b)

The scale of its ambition, the strangeness of the situation and its financial and organizing constraints caused uncertainty to flow through every aspect of its organization.

Finding a Platform – EERA

European integration, new technologies, cultural changes and global interdependence have led to the creation of a tremendous variety of European and international networks, focused on specific objectives. These networks link businesses, communities, research centres, and regional and local authorities. They provide new foundations for integration within the EU and for building bridges to the applicant countries and to the world. They also act as multipliers spreading awareness of the EU and showing policies in action (European Commission, 2001c, p. 18). Into this situation, EERA arrived. Formed out of scientific interests and goodwill, it had to come to terms with a post-comparative European space for education and research. It had to act, and was expected to act, as a network of experts and as a source of information and action in the field of educational research at the moment that a 'vast number of pilot projects, meetings, seminars, and the like' and an 'extensive involvement of administrators of educational systems' (Beukel, 2001, p. 129) had begun to shape European education. A legitimate field of education in the EU, even a 'European Model of Education', had begun to emerge (Hingel, 2001, p. 4).

The strangeness of the situation, combined with an urgency of task in EERA, made the idea of an effective platform paramount. The design and maintenance of a common associational infrastructure space, beginning with the process of developing a common identity for the European educational researcher, with associated skills, resources, networking and events, and enabling them to participate in, or structure, a European educational research space, had occupied EERA Council since 2000. There are several features of the current situation in Europe that this proposal was designed to explore and overcome: new ways of organizing and networking across Europe in key subject areas; establishing a sophisticated communicative space, with expanded services; sharing scientific work in educational research; supporting collegiality, intensive review and evaluation; investigating open access effects and new areas of dissemination.

Since the late 1990s, EERA has grown in stability as an 'association of associations' of educational researchers in Europe. The number of national associations represented on its Council has grown; it has a series of well-organized annual conferences, a large growth in active research-based networks and has established its own journal for European educational researchers (with over two thousand subscribers). It has reduced its overheads and increased its office effectiveness. By the standards of a well-organized national association, it is successful. Yet, within a few years, it had to overcome a relocation of its offices and paid staff, fluctuating income and loss of archive data. It is probably true to argue that if a problem needs special resources, such as expertise in technological development or substantial investment in electronic communication software, it is harder for the EERA Council or its office staff to manage its solution. It would be hard in a national association also, but there is a sense in which bounded associations, with a history of working in territories and with institutions, can manage their tasks better through closely related networks of academics and known procedures, than EERA could. Complex problems are much harder to manage in what is, in effect, a virtual network with communications spread across time zones, and diverse spaces and systems. In this category of problem would be enhanced communications with members, a pressing issue bedevilled by the fact that there are no clear membership lists, from each constituent association, communication expertise and resources are not easily available, and a website built on an integrated database would need new investment.

When voluntary EERA officers are also trying to manage conference agreements, budgets and large-scale paper submissions, alongside their senior academic tasks nationally, this kind of chore is hard to accomplish. But, looking back over the years, the task set by its own strategy document of the late 1990s, that of a steady engagement with, and the increasing effectiveness of, partnerships in Europe has been a major disappointment. There is a limit to the organizing capacities a professional association is capable of managing when stretched across heterogeneous networks of culture, academic context, system history, and low finance, even with goodwill, high purpose and well-intentioned enthusiasm.

Idea of the Space and the Platform

The problem of creating a stable 'platform' stayed with EERA constantly. At first, this was a problem of people and technology, and then, a problem of managing ambition. From the 1990s, EERA wanted to have a professional development function (i.e. disseminating new methodological procedures, such as statistical modelling techniques and computer-based qualitative research systems), a policy function (developing ideas and a policy document on research ethics or on quality in educational research) or meetings that bring together researchers and policy makers on specific current areas of education.

From its foundation, the EERA's Council was concerned with the issue of communicating with its members, mainly the members in the national associations. It had organized a Bulletin or Newsletter from 1994 and this needed editors, agreed content and clear distribution. Even when the Bulletin could be produced well, it did not go to individual members, except in the case of one association. Following a weak financial situation after the ECER in Frankfurt in 1997, the high costs of production and the limited distribution of the Bulletin, this element of the platform came under review. An EERA website was constructed in 1998 and within a short time, the website was seen as a major new resource for European researchers. An EERA Network saw the use of the Internet as a means of offering structured access to information on educational research and of stimulating communication across the research community by exploiting the capability of the Internet (e.g. specialised links of sources, discussion forum, bulletin boards, address board, hypertext links, etc.). By 2007, a database, connected to this site, contained 7500 ECER presentations in its online catalogue and 898 full text papers, with a profile of gradually increasing download of files (from 1600 downloads in 2000 to 24,000 in 2008).

Ordering an association into existence was one major and continuing task, but there were others. From the beginning of EERA, it was intended that it would act within the field of European educational research and one of the Council's first acts was to encourage a key Council member to create an ambitious survey of national associations across Europe about the condition of educational research in their countries, which was followed by a presidential symposium, 'Changing Conditions and Governance of Education Research in Europe', in the 1999 ECER:

> a more international and differentiated view of how educational research is organized and funded in different national contexts, and what changes or reforms in education systems imply for education research. Hopefully this will lead to increased possibilities for international research and cooperation and integration in Europe. (Secretary General, EERA Archive, 1999, unpublished note)

It was intended that the ECER would act as a place in which organized discussion and analysis of European research issues would continue and a discussion of European organizational and policy issues fostered (Gretler, 1999a, 2007). 'Council, through its officers, should organize events within ECER itself to make sure that European policy on research is understood and analyzed' (EERA Review 1998-2001, President/ Secretary General, EERA Archive, 2001). Some years later, in 1986, an EU research infrastructure bid was produced to assist EERA to become a strong foundation for research within Europe.

Using the EERA as an example, and it is possible it is not an exemplar, then the Europeanization process in education research had some problems. The first, on foundation, was that neither EERA, nor the people who came to its meetings, were clear what a European Association was. Secondly, the policy space it was trying to act within began to change rapidly after 2001 and it was difficult to keep abreast of developments, and to respond. Thirdly, the platform it was trying to establish was to be based upon a stable office and finances, and this began to happen only a few years ago (2008) after a long struggle. Many of these problems were overcome by the use of new communication technologies that came into being in the first years of the new millennium which enabled faster and more sophisticated links with its networks and conference.

The existence of an embryo European association has effects in the policy space it was loosely embedded in; for example, it was consulted irregularly by the European Commission, and national associations came into being and rapidly engaged in this common European project. But as its understanding of the complexities of the EU and its operations grew, it became frustrated by its inability to influence it, especially over the question of research infrastructure in Europe, and with its early dependence on outside funding to realize its aims. This frustration began to decrease as its own discretionary funding increased and members became more successful with linked proposals.

While the associational mode of governing, part of a wider soft governance, was difficult to ascertain at times, the EERA did come to rely on the willingness and ability of its members to engage with each other, and the goodwill they showed to the confusions of the Association's tasks. EERA's platform, based on the ability of European educational researchers to come together, and supported by a new platform technology, was internally focused for many years and it took some years before it could work externally, on the ideas and strategies of the European education research policy space. EERA supported a project from one of its own networks (with EU funding) intended to create a multilingual database of Internet resource descriptions; to aid the promotion and dissemination of information about educational research activity; and to create a collection of information about Internet resources through designated national agencies. The idea of a European Social Science Citation Index was mooted (in 2004) and, in 2007, a project 'to build a repository for European educational research documents'.

From its earliest days, EERA conceived of its task as supporting, ordering and arranging its members through the work of its Office. It implicitly and explicitly felt that it represented in this task the expression of European ideas, skills and interests in educational research, through interest and expert based exchanges. It was working with the grain of its own interests (as it was coming to realize them) and the way the EU worked. It did not find its platform easy to assemble.

Conclusion

The professional European imaginary, explored here through associations, actors and networks, is still persuasive, offering room for engagement and interpretation. But governing has become tighter as well. Post Lisbon, it is helpful now to analyse this policy space as it is used more and more as a descriptor of what is being produced by benchmarking, comparison and re-categorization across systems.

This Europeanization of education 'space' can be examined through a linking of social structures, networks and actors at the local, national and European levels and in turn, may reveal the formation of new European identities within emergent policy networks. The range of actors, their spaces of work and deliberation, their forms of engagement can no longer be described as an elite of policy makers nor as an extended and distributed form of policy making or even as a work within non-binding policy areas. They may be working to produce a new area of meaning, a regional imaginary in Laïdi's sense; they are attracted to this

European space yet varying in their contributions, their expertise, their purposes and their opportunities. As an area of governance, it may not be visible or even disciplining to its members, who are nevertheless creating it. Examples might be: a statistician travelling across borders from university to university for expert group meetings on indicators, referring to it as just 'working with a network of academics in her area', and yet producing a crucial element in the formation of the benchmarking process; or members of a lifelong learning network, which is high in sociality and low in productivity in its short life, but from which two members establish later a European association sub-network in a growing common area of work. In both cases, they are contributing to the foundation of a new space of policy in education, and building it by a series of necessary but almost invisible steps. Even the dominance of a sociality in their efforts, rather than some solid product, is really, judged from within studies of the new discourses of production, providing the semblance of solidarity and denying strangeness, the basis of future production of action (Casey, 1995).

Governance is a new paradigm, representing a shift from hierarchy and state hierarchies, and referring to a set of institutions and actors that are drawn from, but also beyond, government. The legitimacy of governing authority cannot be demanded but has to be negotiated and its relation with its partners in civil society is one of steering, guiding and contracting, within recognition that supported networks are unstable and fluctuating. It is the new imaginary, produced to attract, with few levers of control, and populated by actors who attempt to colonize it. So, a broad policy space in education is emerging, and it is being formed through cultural and market influences, supported or associational networking (Cram, 1998), integrated networks of experts and direct European Commission action, including contracts, policy documents and initiatives. European networking is a soft power tool for the enabling of the governance of Europe, attracting and producing opportunities for the growth of meaning about it, necessary for its production and governance.

A wide range of partners are at work, at different levels of government, spanning producer, professional and expert forms, and representing highly organized sectors, like higher education or specialist academic associations. They are often funded directly by the EU and its programmes or indirectly by professional associations and national organizations (like universities). Non-territorial, horizontal networks, involving actors drawn from outside governmental organizations, are visibly at work, creating a space around their interests and trying to overcome problems of legitimacy. They appear to be self-governing networks of actors mobilizing capacities for action, appearing autonomous yet often relying, at some level, on governmental power. To create and manage policy, a range of partners, at different levels of government, has to be negotiated with; they exist within complex networks, which span intergovernmental, producer, professional and expert forms. The European Union 'provides sub national actors with additional resources and a 'philosophy of governance based on cooperative governing which changes their ideas about how efficient governance can be achieved' (Borzel, 1997, p. 9). Increasingly, it appears that networks, woven into sets of linked relations, represent a common form of governance in Europe, crossing national boundaries, old government divisions and traditions of work and administration. The informality of their organization, the complexity of their knowledge relations and exchanges, the hybridity of their institutional association, combined with their overall interdependence, produce a distinctive form of governance in Europe.

They have been portrayed as producing new strategic geographies, enhanced by network technologies, through which civic and public partners, from cities to universities, bypassing their national states, are producing a complex infrastructure. Network governance operates within a rich matrix of flows and scapes, and on different scales, involving actors pulled in through partnerships, associated initiatives, professional innovations and manager networking, all connected by funding searches, performance improvement and interest. It has been argued that

> policy-making in the EU takes place in a highly dynamic, complex and diversified environment where public actors at both the European and the national level are increasingly dependent on the resources of public subnational (regional and local governments) as well as private actors of all territorial levels (transnational, national, subnational interest groups etc.) Hierarchical co-ordination either through the Commission or the national governments has become inefficient. (Borzel, 1997, p. 12)

In effect, academics and experts, often through their associations, act as new political actors. They are the transmitters and mediators of European Union or European socialization logics, ranging from new procedures, and institutional priorities, to networking discourses, and their associational identities and strategies. Professional associations are becoming crucial in the governance of many areas of EU policy, especially ICT (Knill, 2001), where they act to provide expertise in areas where the European Commission is weak, and where intervention involves a range of heterogeneous actors. Associations have begun to alter their structures, from federalist and national, to European and individual membership, to cope with the new demands upon them in providing expertise, acting as policy mediators between the national and the transnational, and supporting ambitious European goals. Even education is not immune from this as European-wide associations struggle to achieve for their members information and influence, and cope with Commission expectations about their stability and expertise. They engage with a range of supported (partially or wholly funded) networking arising out of the new governance of Europe (regions, transnational programmes, EU Declarations, etc.) and related funding (through Socrates, thematic networks, EU-based research projects, benchmarking work groups, etc.).

All the time, they struggle to understand the complexities of the policy space they are in, the relation between the national and the European, and the establishing of a platform, metaphorically and practically, in which to engage. Their members may be supported in many ways, through European and national networks of expertise, and professional development interest areas, and as their associations grow, they become more susceptible to governance. Indeed, their struggle for good service to members may make them even more linked into European discourses and actions.

CHAPTER 5

Governance by Experts and Standards?

> Walter Hallstein, the first president of the Commission, stated in 1955 that the EU could not be the work of experts, but that it had to rest upon the unity of the peoples of Europe themselves. (Petit, 2007, p. 2, quoting Bossuat, 1994)

Through the construction of European policy spaces, the European Union makes Europe governable. The gradual emergence of the European education policy space, and its centrality in contemporary European policy, the subject of this book, is not just a question of substantive policy direction but a question of European governance. The means and acts of governing in Europe appear to be particular to it, and are reflections of the problems of diverse statist jurisdictions, network organization, market solutions and politics. The field of education is one element in this governing problematic and it appears to be represented by soft governance, the use of persuasive power (Lawn, 2006), expert influence and an instrumentalization of new forms of non-state power to govern 'at a distance' (Miller & Rose, 2008, p. 205). As education was originally a sensitive area of policy, where hard regulation would infringe national sovereignty, there was always a politics in this policy area. This has been overcome with the use of experts, a precise focus on the creation of data through common tools and categories (Ozga et al, 2011), and their production of standards, through networked processes and technological innovation. Expert and standardizing processes in European governing are part of a persuasive and attracting power which draws actors in, across a range of levels, places and spaces, to community engagement (Lawn, 2006). The new education actor may be an ICT consultant, developing content for a new e-learning platform, or an academic, specializing in indicators, or a school improvement professional. In effect, these experts are engaged in producing new European standards on learning platforms, indicators or school quality, which will become interoperable or consistent across Europe. Actors move from country to country and site to site, and they take with them this expertise and system knowledge, and new platforms enable standards, their codified knowledge, to be shared between research institutes, schools, and the national and European level.

Expertise has changed over the years. Originally, it was embedded in key professors of education, aware of each other across borders, and associated with comparative study and measurement. Research knowledge and experience became codified, and allowed the community of experts to be widened. The production and use of standards across the whole range of education policy created an apparently 'loose' form of governing in which 'professional and organizational knowledge-practices are reinvented in increasingly formalized, universalized and standardized ways' (Higgins & Larner, 2010, p. 1).

So, a new governing architecture of public and private experts and other actors built European education through arrays of interlocking standards. Governing by standards excludes politics and relies on experts while offering workable solutions to governing and being governed in Europe. Since the 1990s, the governing of European education has depended on the production of abstract and commensurable units, enabling exchange across borders and places, and producing a newly transparent domain. Standards work to bring into being and shape the social world and its subjects, and make them governable. They allow coordination across organizations and agents, which makes new systems work (Dale, 2009). Standards created by new experts produce:

> orienting relations between political society (via the administrative executive) and civil society (via its administered subjects) through intermediaries in the form of devices that mix technical components (measuring, calculating the rule of law, procedure) and social components (representation, symbol). (Lascoumes & Le Galès, 2007, p. 6)

The production of standards in the EU has been developed by inclusive, expert and technical processes, such as networking, seminars, reviews, expert groups, etc. It has produced an intertwined and captivated Europeanized population of experts, practitioners and professionals, and especially so within the field of education. Its virtue is that power is not wielded; if anything, it aims to attract, and uses 'incentive acts' (Brunsson & Jacobsson, 2000, p. 13). This form of expert power involves whole series and networks of private and public experts, some close to policy decision making, and others acting at a distance. As in the production of open source software, they benefit from working together, at different speeds, times and places, to strengthen and develop a common policy, over time, built upon commensurability. The value of expert power, codified and circulated by them, is that it excludes politics, produces predictability and creates a sort of governing without government. At the same time, it appears to leave the national systems and their governance alone while harmonizing systems and building the European policy space.

Governing by expertise is crucial then. Experts from different epistemic communities, with diverse roles and knowledge, including reflexive knowledge about their work in Europe, are threaded through reports of meetings, project reports, conferences and seminars and the EU's different directorates. Experts abound; with varied contracts of employment or consultancy, and with varied or no national experience of policy. They work for agencies, broker agents, mediating companies, public–private partnerships, consultancy firms, and even directly for the Directorates-General themselves. The ubiquity of experts in governing Europe means that an initial caution about their role has been overlooked in creating coherent policy spaces.

Using Experts

The term 'expert' is ubiquitous in the field of EU education, starting with the Janne report in 1972, which was devised around the responses of senior scholars, researchers and other European actors, and which foreshadowed a European Community education policy.

> Over the 20 years preceding Community involvement in the field of education, a pattern and a culture of cooperation thus developed within the framework of the Council of Europe between the Member States and also between European experts in the field and with non-governmental organisations representing the interests of the education sector and civil society. (Pépin, 2006, p. 51)
> The Education Committee ... also regularly supported many organisations and associations working at European level (teachers' unions, student and other organisations). Various working groups were set up consisting of national experts and stakeholders, giving them the opportunity to share best practice and experience. (Pépin, 2006, p. 36)

Experts were needed to explain how to overcome 'training problems' in 1971 (Pépin, 2006, p. 94), and in 1977:

> four working groups created to cover education and vocational training met for the first time to make cooperation arrangements. They decided to set up one single group for statistics on education and vocational training, composed of experts from the national statistical offices, the ministries of education and the ministries of employment and social affairs. (Pépin, 2006, p. 82)

The 1993 White Paper on growth, competitiveness and employment produced a focus on the challenges facing European education and training systems. A study group was set up in September 1995 to gather the opinions of independent experts (Pépin, 2006, p. 160). In 1998 the European Commission set up a group of national experts, appointed by the ministers of education, to identify a limited number of indicators of the quality of school education (Pépin, 2006, p. 196; European Commission, 2001d). They continued their work and produced a second report for the European education ministers in Bratislava in 2002, this time on 15 quality indicators for lifelong learning (Pépin, 2006, p. 197). That year, the Commission set up a standing group on indicators and benchmarks to advise on a vital component of the open method of coordination (OMC) – how to use and develop reliable and relevant indicators to monitor the process up to 2010. This group consisted of experts nominated by the Member States, and this can be taken as a sign of the increased use of experts, especially technical experts, in the European governance created by the adoption of the OMC. When the major Socrates programme was evaluated in 2001, it was already being monitored by a group of 'experts appointed by the Member States and representatives of European associations in the field of education' (Pépin, 2006, p. 177).

When the Commission published an Action Plan for Skills and Mobility in 2002, it was based upon the work of 'a high-level task force set up by the European Commission and consisting of experts from business, the educational world and the social partners' (Pépin, 2006, p. 215). In 2004, the Commission set up a high-level group of independent experts to help it prepare a mid-term review of the Lisbon Strategy at the European Council for the following year (Pépin, 2006, p. 223).

Temporary expert groups have mutated into permanent forms of Europe's governance approach. Since 2000, the President has had a special group of policy advisers, part of whose duties is to work with leading political scientists and researchers. It works with external advisory groups – involving experts from the fields of economics, politics and social science:

> The overall objective is to stimulate an ongoing dialogue
> between the European Commission and European experts from
> academia, business and civil society and to provide President
> Barroso and Commissioners with objective, expert and
> impartial advice in the formulation of recommendations on
> policies of the European Union. (Group of Political Analysis,
> 2012)

> Expert groups are to a considerable extent populated by
> national representatives with or without a mandate.

> Directorate General Research is particularly strong in
> mobilizing expert groups. Nobody knows how many expert
> groups are in existence at a given moment and the numbers
> obviously fluctuate. Estimates of current numbers are
> 800-1300. (Mamadouh & Van der Wusten, 2008, p. 28)

In recent years, the numbers of experts who have become seconded from national contexts, such as ministries, to work in the Directorate-General for Education and Culture have increased significantly. These experts have a sense of the political project they are engaged in, and their close and continuing links with their national base.

> One of the Commission officials expressed the view that
> Member States were constantly monitoring the Commission to
> ensure that it was not building up a critical mass of education
> policy experts. To an extent, DG EAC [Directorate-General for
> Education and Culture] was able to circumvent this restriction
> by appointing Temporary Commission Officials with
> significant education policy expertise and by benefiting from
> the increased willingness of national level civil servants to
> become Seconded National Experts. (Jones, 2010, p. 76)

These embedded experts assist policy makers in the preparation of working documents to support the European Commission's directives and recommendations. They attend meetings and symposia organized by the DG-EAC but they are not involved in the policy process during the different phases of trade-offs with national administrations, European Parliament or interest groups.

> In addition, European policy makers mobilize informal
> networks to develop scientific knowledge about the
> effectiveness and quality of educational systems. This
> expertise contributes to the construction of indicators and
> benchmarks supporting the open method of coordination. This
> knowledge is very useful for the European Commission, which
> looks for efficiency in the implementation of its strategy of
> lifelong learning, while member states retain the control of
> their national systems in education and training. (Normand,
> 2010, p. 407)

For example, following the establishment of an organized group of economists advising DG-EAC, the Network of Experts in Social Sciences of Education and Training (NESSE) was set up by tender in 2007. Its purpose was to advise and support the European Commission in the analysis of educational policies and reforms, and to consider their implications at national, regional and European level. It also disseminated information about the social aspects of education and training. The purpose of the expert group was focused on social justice, and education and training; the experts were expected to aid the policy group, the permanent group within DG-EAC, in their planning and knowledge base. The tension they worked within was between the knowledge economy targets on economic growth and education, and Europe (and DG-EAC's) social aims on a just, equitable education system. It is not clear if the embedded experts in DG-EAC were able to act as a bridge between policy and research in the difficult relations between these areas. NESSE produced Brussels seminars on a range of useful (and requested) subjects: for example, on creativity and innovation, equality and social exclusion, school failure, and migration. NESSE's experts were called upon frequently to provide information for DG-EAC. In one reported case, seeking assistance with a conference on the secondary analysis of international studies:

> The feedback we received from colleagues in Unit A4 ... is very positive. Colleagues found the reply very useful in several ways, especially for the selection of the various topics to be addressed at the conference and for their grouping. The reply included information on some researchers that we did not have on our radar who could be invited as participants or speakers/keynote speakers at the conference. The list of studies and researchers (sent as an annex) was useful. (Centre Director's Annual Report, 2008/9 – Learning and Life Chances in Knowledge Economies and Societies [LLAKES])

The relationship between the experts and the policy groups might be expressed as taking the form of a rational exchange, overlain with technical expertise. In a discussion of expert networks and policy, Normand describes the way that European policy makers cloak their work:

> In explaining the process of Europeanization in education policies, I have preferred to insist on the expertise which naturalizes decision making which presents itself as neutral and universal. This position displays a particular representation which gives us the impression that policy makers manage public action with method and rationality. This rhetoric is effective because instruments of measurement are considered as a proof of scientific objectivity. Expertise also helps to elaborate a common vision of public issues in education so the Commission can act as an entrepreneur in the area of lifelong learning without risking any intrusion in the affairs of states. (Normand, 2010, p. 415)

Ideas Brokers

In a decentred, information-rich society, governance needs to use 'science' more actively to minimize risk, or to minimize anxiety about risk (Baumann, 1992). So, new technocratic actors constitute a new EU policy instrument that knits together a complex space of flows of agents and data, with the aim of imposing its logic over scattered, segmented places and producing a governing knowledge value from them.

By brokers we mean those who influence the decision-making process and create institutions; to do this, ideas must be linked, associated or conveyed from one field to another. This has been described as mobilizing the 'distributed intelligence' of multilevel, multi-actor deliberations and pooling it into public goods available on the network (Tucker, 2003, p. 15). Ideas brokers perform the role of conveying ideas between different areas of the production, distribution or circulation of ideas. Ideas brokers could include opinion researchers, media and experts in public relations who advocate policy programmes, and, for example, experts who link paradigms and programmes (international experts working with the OECD, the EU, etc.; consultants); think tanks and policy institutes; business and trade organisations. Ideas brokers are useful to the European Commission, which 'lacks the formal leadership role it has in the Community method, (so) it must strive to acquire informal influence ... based on technical expertise and its knowledge of policy issues' (Tucker, 2003, p. 15).

Since the OMC began, 'hybrid' experts committee have been created that 'fuse' supranational and intergovernmental experts into a consultative body for the European Council and European Commission. These committees hold non-public meetings roughly every month, which are supposed to facilitate the mutual learning processes by incorporating expertise into the OMC processes. Although they have no formal power, the depoliticized deliberations encourage a free exchange of ideas, and build trust between the Commission and Member State experts (Tucker, 2003, p. 7).

In a study by Grek et al of the rise of data to manage systems in education, interviews took place with actors who may be classified as 'brokers'; that is, people who are located in some sense at the interface between the national and the European and who 'translate' the meaning of national data into policy terms in the European arena and who also interpret European developments in the national space. The interviews focused on the production and use of data, working within the discourse of successful competition, high quality and standards. These policy actors 'interpret their brokering as a fusion of European and global influences that places pressure on systems to demonstrate success in terms of measurable outcomes' (Grek et al, 2009b, p. 7).

These policy 'brokers' occupy a dual role between and within national systems and the European or transnational agencies and organizations involved in producing or collecting quality indicators in education. In each national system, therefore, Grek et al identified key personnel (policy and data analysts, people with responsibility for the national implementation of PISA testing, school inspectors with a European remit and so on, as well as members of Brussels-based organizations with a relevant role in national systems) and conducted semi-structured interviews with them about their positioning, their membership of networks, and their views about data flows and comparability (Grek et al, 2009b, p. 10).

The governance of the European education policy space appears from the data as being increasingly 'done' through building relations between people – groups/nations in networks/communities. The project of Europeanization seems increasingly dependent upon the cooperation and joint resource mobilization of national policy actors who sometimes lie outside governmental hierarchical control. Further, policy networks accommodate the blurring of state/civil society boundaries that is such a feature of current policy-making – perhaps especially in England – with the growth of cooperation or dispersed responsibilities among state and non-state agencies, and engagement of actors from the private and voluntary sectors in the delivery of services. The term 'policy community' (Rhodes, 1996) denotes a network with high levels of stability and continuity, longer-term agendas and interests beyond the sectoral- or issue-based (Grek et al, 2009b, p. 13).

The discourse is one of *translation*; uneven in influence and effect, these system actors move between Brussels and the home state, and between states, interpreting one to the other, and easing the path of change. They act as translators between sites, turning information into powerful knowledge, re-imagining the project of Europe and repositioning the national. This powerful role, acting as symbolic analysts, depends for its effect upon the central or peripheral status of their country in Europe; they might have greater or lesser influence and be the bearer of powerful or weak discursive effects, depending on the positioning of the country in relation to the EU project. They circulate an explicit language of comparison and evaluation, new generic skills and 'learning' which, although of wider international usage than specifically 'European', appear in particular forms in the Europeanizing space. The system actors cannot offer an unambiguous vision of a 'workable future' but only the necessity to modernize to cope with the 'ordinary present'. This might have disruptive effects in peripheral countries and yet be normative in others.

The system actors circulate and translate an explicit language of collection, comparison and evaluation, and of new generic skills and 'learning' which, although of wider international usage than specifically 'European', appears in particular forms in the Europeanizing space. Europeanization appears to be the means by which larger visions are projected or demanded and in which a 'workable future' can be conceived. However, while 'difference' is the new international watchword, Europe offers the chance to produce meaning and not just results, purpose and productivity. At the same time, it is used to 'modernize' and even enforce modernization, a task that the system actors try to manage, shuttling between sites.

Building a System through Standards

A defining aspect of the European education policy space is that it has to be governable and unobtrusive, and so to harmonize without regulation has always been the approach taken. As the audit state develops (Power, 1999), the gathering of information, the evaluation of systems, organizations and people, and the formation of valid judgements about purposes and practices are increasing (Busch, 2007, p. 1). It is argued that there is:

> a veritable explosion in the quantity and scope of standards.
> For governments, private companies and non-governmental
> organizations standards offer a new way to govern. Even a shift
> in our use of language, from government to governance, is
> indicative of this change. (Busch, 2007, p. 6)

A range of actors and experts have worked in cooperation with the EU, national agencies and commercial companies to produce a constantly developing range of standards across the field of education and learning since 2000. The key word driving the production of standards is interoperability – each part must connect to and enable the other; each actor or object must trust or be trusted. The interoperability of systems (through their standardized components or procedures) is a constant process – of negotiation, of audit and market judgement. Europe is growing in strength because of its ability to create, define, construct and govern by standards; it does this by a constant process of building in small improvements, derived from performance monitoring and comparison, which build interoperability through these new standardized components.

> For governments, standards offer an opportunity for
> deregulation and improved governance as they help to reduce
> the level of regulatory detail to the essential requirements
> needed to attain legitimate objectives such as the protection of
> health, safety and the environment. (Ayral, 2005, p. 3)

So, the EU has created a lightly steered, flexible, low-regulation system in Europe, by encouraging a negotiated harmonization. To do this, it delegates the task to experts in quality or standards associations, and private companies. Standards have shifted from being descriptive specifications of objects into performance requirements, checked through systematic quality management. As Europe moves forward, these standards are used within technologies and systems to enable a greater convergence to occur. Each part must work with the next one so that the system can be built and players can trust and exchange. This process does not require legislation; it is simple, flexible and effective (Ayral, 2005, pp. 7-9).

The field of education is itself less visible and less contentious; it is amorphous, it is not owned, it is normative and it has many actors. These actors are producing the policy space in education in quiet ways, through their presence and influence in their interest groups, business and knowledge-based elites on policy processes and outcomes.

Many actors involved in standardizing activities in education treat them as academic, specialist, logical, normative, helpful or interesting. They do not see them as extending a form of state power or colluding in a covert European politics and policy. It can be argued that standards have not the fixedness of past times, and are rather fluid, relative and performance based. They fit closely with the EU policy of soft governance: a lightly regulated, persuasive and self-managing form of governing in which policy is depoliticized. Soft governance relies on negotiation, persuasion and 'voluntarily' agreed performance. So it is in the field of education and learning.

Assembling a Learning Space: data and platforms

Education as a policy space has been translated into 'learning', and lifelong learning, supported by e-learning, has reconstituted education, widening the field, integrating its functions, centring the individual learner and stressing performance and comparison.

Major processes of standardizing European education have taken place through the production of benchmarks and indicator data through the EU's own centres of calculation (see later) or by the continuous stitching together, through standards, of cross-border platforms. For example, ECTS, the European Credit Transfer and Accumulation System in higher education, created a common standard, the credit, consisting of the learning outcome and its workload time, which has enabled student mobility between institutions and countries, and a market between institutions, based on trusted, common standards. At the same time, data is produced on mobility, achievement, hot spot sites and weak performance. The growth of the European Qualifications Framework, built upon the closely interlinked national frameworks arising across Europe, is another example of standardization in the way it seeks to improve the 'transparency, comparability and portability' of qualifications in the European Union (Cort, 2010).

Lifelong learning has turned from being a useful idea at the turn of century, into a data-mapped area and then a mobilized field of action and comparison as it became a central part of knowledge economy goals. Turning this new policy objective, lifelong learning, into a governable policy space meant that a new EU area of education (integrated with employment, economic growth and social exclusion), needed to have its data categories for collection and comparison developed and re-standardized; they had to be made comparable between different fields of government and between national systems. A European Commission resolution emphasised the significance of information sharing between Member States and the need for education statistics. Eurostat had begun to publish data, based on national statistics, since 1978; nonetheless, it was only after the 1990s that it began producing more statistically comparable data. According to the Commission, 'the objective was not to create new indicators in such a short time but to identify the quality-related problems which were politically most relevant for European countries, and then determine which of the existing indicators, drawn mainly from Eurostat, the OECD, the IEA and Eurydice, could shed most light on these problems' (European Commission, 2006a, pp. 196-197). Thus, the contribution of the different data agencies towards establishing appropriate benchmarks was taken for granted right from the start. Indicators were not devised from scratch, but were constituted on the basis of triangulating existing data that at this point were deemed useful; in a sense, most of the work towards establishing the new quality assurance in education framework for European education was already in place. What was necessary was to coordinate data, organizations and minds towards the requirements of the new knowledge economy. So, in 2000, a task force on lifelong learning and statistical data was created, which epitomizes our argument about standards governance, networks and direction. The task force involved several Directorates-General (Education and Culture, Employment and Social Affairs, Research, EuroStat), several Member-State national statistical agencies, European agencies (the European Centre for the Development of Vocational Training and the European Unit of Eurydice) and the OECD and UNESCO (European Commission, 2001a, p. 5). After this first mapping of EU human capital and its relation to employment, and education and training policy, the EU found that it needed a wider range and better quality of statistical data on adult learning, in order to inform policy making, policy monitoring and benchmarking activities. National data needed to be harmonized to make more national initiatives in this field, as part of the Lisbon Strategy: so, this task force on measuring lifelong learning (2000-2001) was succeeded by a task force on adult education (2002-4) (European Commission, 2005d), which also used existing sources of data learning including the EU Labour Force Survey and the Continuous Vocational Training Survey.

Between 2005 and 2008, the Adult Education Survey (AES) carried out surveys in 29 countries in the EU and candidate countries. The first AES was a pilot exercise, which then proposed a common EU framework including a standard questionnaire, tools and reporting on quality. Taking place every five years, the AES now covers participation in education and lifelong learning activities (formal, non-formal and informal learning) of all Europeans between the ages of 25 and 64. Participation rates, obstacles to learning, reasons for participation, instruction hours spent, costs, non-participation, etc. are all viewable now, and open to further governance. Integration of data was followed by mapping national policies at European level, then a further more detailed mapping, and then linked Lisbon benchmarking standards; in this way, a policy space comes into being and governance is established. It is continual: major statistical conferences involving state and commercial partners, with Eurostat, are held regularly to harmonize statistical standards (e.g. Statistics for Policymakers: Europe 2020, in Brussels, in March 2010).

Experts, data and standards have created a common trading language in education and learning in Europe: for example:

> The Commission, the Member States and social partners will jointly examine the role and character of minimum quality standards in education and training. The development of such standards, accompanied by a peer-review approach, would increase the transparency and coherence of national education systems, creating a basis for mutual trust and recognition of qualification (European Commission, 2001e, p. 16)

A key component in this process is the use of standardized software platforms, combining new initiatives and advanced technology, created through networks linked to hubs. The process of establishing standards that support and control the actions of institutional participants, for example, can be seen in two snapshots: firstly, about the standardization of inter-school networking across Europe, and secondly, through a series of testing and evaluation projects, viewed through an association, the European Distance and E-Learning Network (EDEN).

As we have seen, the European Schoolnet was originally a way of linking up virtual, national cultural sites into a single site accessible by schools across Europe, and was tasked to set up a model platform through which new multimedia tools could be developed and validated. The Schoolnet encouraged schools to work with each other, and one of its sub-projects has been on school twinning (to work together on curriculum projects, exchange of materials, etc.) which, by 2008, had 35,000 schools in virtual school partnerships. Even a process like twinning schools together in Europe became part of a European standardizing process. First, a national quality label was awarded by the national support services to schools whose work, within an eTwinning partnership, was considered to be excellent. Schools have to be awarded their national quality label to achieve the European standard (the European Quality Label). With an EQL, a school may be judged a reliable and trusted partner by other European schools. A whole series of Schoolnet application and award procedural standards had been produced since 2006, but criteria about, for example, a European dimension, curricular integration, sustainability, and use of ICT, were later devised to achieve the EQL. In this way, standards of operation become ubiquitous. Schoolnet soon metamorphosed into a major hub for the new learning infrastructure, and a permanent workshop mixing teachers, school managers, infrastructure suppliers, commercial hardware vendors, content developers and standards bodies. Another example of the constant creation of standard platforms of e-learning, underpinning the flexible lifelong learning policy area, is the associational hub, the European Distance and E-Learning Network (EDEN), founded in the early 1990s, but galvanized by the knowledge society movement and the 'unprecedented opportunities' for ICT learning initiatives. EDEN's newsletters show how a standard learner information package is being produced, through a process of bricolage: EDEN-supported projects include work on professional learning for adults on the move; social e-learning environments; technologies for networking and international collaboration; the European mobile worker's kit; megatrends in e-learning provision; and electronic authentication of e-learning. In this way, the policy area materializes. Learning Europe became the production of the sustaining software and advanced technologies able to extend the local practices of lifelong learning inside the EU and outside it.

The learner, at the home or the workplace, needed common formats, a consistency of description and the same metadata. They lacked 'international and national standards and guidelines, inspection systems, quality awards, financial instruments' (European Commission, 2001e, p. 14). This became known as the problem of Learning Object Metadata, the standards which should apply to learning objects, that is, multimedia technologies, instructional or course content, and software tools. The Learning Interoperability Framework for Europe (LIFE), funded by DG-EAC and managed by Schoolnet, is just one of the projects working to determine common standards in e-learning. Without interoperability, it will not be possible for e-learning to 'share, collaborate, twin, and move people and resources across Europe' (European Schoolnet, 2006, p. 1).

> Project partners were tasked with providing information on
> national policies and good practice examples on common
> user-friendly e-platforms;

more effective and efficient lifelong learning services as institutions seek to improve their standards;

the validation of informal and non-formal learning through the use of a general methodological tool is to be also tried and tested in a number of jobs in different sectors across Europe. (European Commission, 2008)

The assembling of a policy area in virtual and material form, enabled by public and private actors, and hybrids of the two, with its own means of calculation, categories and standards, has moved very fast in the last 10 years.

Final Point

Our approach to Europeanization views the EU as actively constructing European spaces which it is capable of governing at a distance. Governing aims to impose its logic over scattered, segmented places (Castells, 1996) and to produce a disciplining and enabling space of engagement with state and transnational agencies and elites. The effect is to create a thick tapestry of communication, organizational and network relations, stable and unstable linkages, and career patterns and constructed networked spaces which can subsequently be organized as sites of European governance. These sites of engagement constitute the field of European networking in education, and contain both traditional actors in the field of education (institutional policy makers, university groupings, organized professional interests) and those conventionally considered peripheral to education governance (commercial interests, networks of participation and interest, technological innovators). Governing this space occurs not just through agents, data, discourse or regulation, but also by standards. Standards are quintessential policy instruments. Building on agreed standards helps to create and extend the policy spaces which are being produced and governed across private and public arenas in new ways. The warp and weft of the European policy space in education is provided by the work of these experts, policy actors and ideas brokers.

CHAPTER 6

Second-Wave Policy in EU Education, 2000-2010

The flow of Europeanization is enhanced and shaped by the indicators and data produced in the construction of Europe as a legible, governable, commensurate policy space. Comparison is a key element of the operation of multinational companies which is managed by numerical data, which has increased in velocity, scale and scope. The enhanced policy influence of Europe in all policy domains including education can be seen as part of the new scalar politics, articulating and responding to globalization (Sassen, 2007).

In this chapter, we are paying particular attention to the way in which the growth of (mainly) quantitative data has shaped the European space for education in the last 10 years or so. Although support for cooperating networks and the use of persuasive soft power are still the hallmarks of the governance of education, this has been overshadowed by the huge rise of calculating and standardizing devices, following on from the open method of coordination. The embrace of European governing has continued but there is a new clarity about its aims, the management of the present and the calculation of the future.

From Education to Learning: the role of data

Despite efforts from the 1970s and until the mid 1990s for the setting of a more coherent European education policy agenda, education had still been largely viewed within the European Union and by most scholarship on the EU as a question of subsidiarity, a responsibility of national governments. The signing of the Lisbon Strategy in 2000 can thus be considered as a key culminating point in the history of education governance in the EU, as education and its role and significance were to set to dramatically change: from now on education would become the key element in the new Knowledge Economy goals of Europe (Jessop et al, 2008). As a consequence, due to the Lisbon Strategy and a number of developments in the immediate years prior to it, *education* shifted from its pre-2000 institutionalized and ordered sequences to become a new fluid, flexible and cross-national phenomenon – that of *learning*.

Redefined as 'learning', it has become the centre of EU policy making, as well as a new field of commercial activity, and an entrepreneurial space – for example, in the marketing of universities and, as we saw in the previous chapter, the push for e-learning. Established ways of understanding the politics or the policies of education are being challenged by the need to see learning as individual choice and responsibility.

This development, in the light of the perspective adopted in this book, is of interest as a formal and deliberate policy in the European Union which shapes 'education' as a field, and which overcomes older barriers and borders to do so. But Europe has also strong influences drawn from global pressures and opportunities which are driven by national economies, separately or in harness in the EU, and their key sectors. Post Lisbon, education has become a visible and transparent sector of the European integration policy.

Education as learning has primarily been framed by the developing movement around evidence-informed and evidence-based policy making (Byrne & Ozga, 2008) and the related production and use of data to develop indicators and benchmarks that are central to quality assurance and improved performance in education. Therefore the focus of this chapter is on the processes through which such data are collected, selected and ordered, and on the negotiations and interactions that surround such processes at national, local and institutional levels of policy making.

European practices in educational evaluation range from inspection, quality assurance and evaluation systems and comparative exchange of information. Traditionally each country has its own way of developing the range and scope of its data about its education systems. When the perspective of the 'national' is used, then, often the cross-national – its histories of interaction and flows of people and data – is excluded. However, expertise, technical advice and agreement on common standards are not solely a new phenomenon; they have a long history and they are not confined to national borders.

We thus understand the activity of data collection to constitute a form of governing, and to connect to changing education governance and shared agendas and governing practices across Europe. Data are flowing across Europe, and data act to constitute and enable a new spatial infrastructure to emerge around education. Data systems are not homogeneous or of equal velocity or consequence, nor are they symmetrical. But data, with their attendant databases, policy officers, experts and meetings, constitute new synapses through which messages of comparison and commensurability (messages about standards, ranking scales, indicators and benchmarks) are passed. These generate what might be called a new nervous system which grows across education and which both perceives its functioning and makes it transparent. Without its own buildings, or a professional corpus or even histories of law and regulation, and with deep asymmetries but increasingly discursive similarities, a European space is being fabricated (Nóvoa & Lawn, 2002).

Data are produced as part of a wider move to a calculus society, a move that has not been consistent in the past but which is now dominant in public sector systems, as it is in the private sector (Segerholm, 2003; Dahler-Larsen, 2005). This fundamental change has been analysed through the metaphors of a quality revolution, the evaluation industry and the audit explosion. However, what are the limits of collecting education data and their interpretation? Is this development connected to actual improvements or is simply the common discourse of improvement a key element in contemporary governance –the new lingua franca of education governance? Has the extension of evaluation from specific projects into broad, institutionalized responses created a demand for more and more expertise in evaluation and its methodologies and techniques? While improvement is the key term for governance, the dysfunctionality of performance measurements or indicators is often masked: those are the unintended side effects that sometimes jeopardize the effectiveness of education systems. The representation of improvement and of quality through data and indicators produces an error in judgement; it conflates quality and its representation. As indicators produce new effects in systems, by concentrating on what can be measured and acted upon, at the expense of what is of value, then the exclusion of an expert voice, expressing questions of value, purpose and democratic intent, is felt more.

State expertise, using its own officers or academic and commercial skill and know-how, seems to be metamorphosing into an international or interlinked expertise in which knowing what to 'borrow' or transfer is more significant than in the past. The significance of 'beyond the border' is still dependent on good intelligence and comparative skills, and knowing what has been proven to be best practice. In contemporary Europe, this also means that a lack of capacity in national educational administration, in the ministries and in research institutes may lead to outsourcing of rational, high-skill and strategic thinking from the national to the supranational level. Cross-border information has never been so important to the national ministries and the supranational agencies and governments. Governing needs data and is legitimated by them. If national governments lose their grip on 'their' education systems, they could be replaced by international and global norms or, in some cases, by more parochial local norms. But how did we get here?

Measuring Europe: Lisbon (2000) and after

As already suggested, post-Lisbon 'learning' and the 'knowledge society' were to become the new dominant discourses in the process of fabricating the space of European education. Even though an interest in measuring educational performance through numerical data was evident as early as the mid 1970s [3], the concepts of indicators and benchmarking received the European education ministers' explicit attention for the first time in 1999 at a conference in Prague. The ministers adopted a resolution with a view to *new* working methods for cooperation in education and training which would increase 'continuity, effectiveness and efficiency of education in Europe' (Council of Europe, 2000a). They stressed the need for a more coherent approach for all European Community action and for a structured framework for political discussion and activities over the coming years. The conference theme focused on the quality of school education; the ministers decided to set up a group of national experts who would devise a list of indicators of quality in school education in Europe. According to the European Commission, 'the objective was not to create new indicators in such a short time but to identify the quality-related problems which were politically most relevant for European countries, and then determine which of the existing indicators – mainly from Eurostat, the OECD, the IEA [4] and Eurydice – could shed most light on these problems' (Pépin, 2006, pp. 196-197). The 16 indicators for quality assurance prepared by the group of experts were not devised from scratch. They were constituted on the basis of triangulating existing data that at this point was deemed to be useful; in a sense, most of the work towards establishing the new quality assurance framework for European education was already in place. What was necessary now was to coordinate data, organizations and minds towards the requirements of the new knowledge economy.

In the field of higher education, the Bologna process (1999) set out to achieve a 'coherent and compatible' European area of higher education by 2010, with the introduction of a simplified system of more transparent and comparable degrees across Europe. This would entail the convergence of national systems under a common framework of bachelor's degrees, master's degrees and doctorates (Corbett, 2005). In addition, the European Credit Transfer and Accumulation System (ECTS), which had already been devised for the needs of the Erasmus programme, had to be taken into account, as well as ensuring the European cooperation in quality assurance. A medium-term action plan was devised for the implementation of the Bologna declaration – the Council of Europe described it as 'the most important and wide-ranging reform of higher education since 1968' (cited in Pépin, 2006, p. 197).

However, the turning point towards an increased interest in setting standards for education systems in Europe was the Lisbon Special European Council of 2000. According to the Presidency conclusions, 'the European Union is confronted with a quantum shift resulting from globalisation and the challenges of a new knowledge-driven economy'

(Council of the European Union, 2000b). Therefore, and as it was famously stated, in order to 'become the most competitive and dynamic knowledge-based economy in the world', the Lisbon European Council set the following targets in relation to education and training for the Member States:

- Increase in per capita investment in human resources;
- Halve the number of 18-24-year-olds with only lower secondary education;
- Create multipurpose local learning centres;
- Establish a European framework for lifelong learning and introduce new skills – IT, foreign languages, technological culture, entrepreneurship and social skills;
- Foster the mobility of students, teachers, training and research staff and create greater transparency in the recognition of qualifications;
- Establish a common European format for curricula vitae.

Apart from setting specific objectives, such as an increased investment in human resources, the establishment of a European framework for lifelong learning and the fostering of educational mobility, the Council also suggested a new style of policy formation, the 'open method of coordination' (OMC) (Council of the European Union, 2000a). Indicators and benchmarking are at the heart of this new policy tool, since OMC was declared as the new 'soft' form of governance.

Nonetheless, apart from establishing new strategic goals and the policy frameworks to push them, the Lisbon European Council was significant for one more reason: it was the first time that the Council promoted the need for European education systems to converge. As already discussed, such dialogue, especially in the fields of lifelong learning, vocational training and higher education, had been long under way. However, the coordination of the European education systems at the level of compulsory schooling was a fairly new endeavour. Indeed, although the Lisbon Agenda was essentially an economic agreement, apart from focusing on employment and the economy (the two more 'traditional' areas for joining efforts in the past), it was also the *education* ministers who were appointed with the mission to achieve the Lisbon goals for 2010.

According to the official European Commission overview of the pre- and post-Lisbon developments, the quantification of certain aspects of school life was regarded as a positive step forward: 'While the setting of quantified targets is not unusual in areas such as employment or the economy, it was a very new and bold step at European level in a field like education. Targets have the merit of being explicit and making it easier to assess the progress made' (Pépin, 2006, p. 208). Whilst numbers are fairly easily collected, they do require a firm basis for comparison and cross-systemic analysis of the data; developing the discourses for the justification of measuring specific indicators and benchmarking would soon come to fulfil this need.

Indeed, a year later, the Education Council asked the Commission to draft a report on 'The Concrete Future Objectives of Education and Training Systems' (Council of the European Union, 2001). The report set out 13 objectives to be achieved by 2010 and, according to the Commission, it was 'the first official document sketching a comprehensive and coherent European approach to national education and training policies in the EU' (European Commission, 2002, quoted in Pépin, 2006, p. 209). It was signed at the Stockholm European Council (which took place on 23 and 24 March 2001) by the Commission and it was agreed that a detailed work programme on how to achieve the new goals would be planned. The objectives came under three strategic goals: education and training in Europe should by 2010, according to the report, become more effective and, with improved quality, more accessible and more open (European Commission, 2002a). The heads of states or governments approved the work programme in 2003 and committed themselves to the new vision for European education: a 'world quality reference' by 2010. It was the first time in the history of the European education space that no reference was made to the common European cultural or educational heritage – the focus now was on a projected image of a competitive and social Europe.

The work programme for 2010 was also the first time when OMC was applied as a governing tool. It involved the measuring of progress against objectives and the exchange of information and good practice. Hence, the added importance which was given to transparency and evaluation would initiate a different kind of coordination of the European education systems. Instead of the 1999 'rolling agenda' of reforms (Pépin 2006), according to the European Commission, the OMC 'has the potential to pave the way for coherent policies in areas such as education where a formal common policy is not appropriate but where enhanced cooperation and mutual learning at European level can add real value' (European Commission, 2002b, p. 16). In other words, alongside the old methods of networking and exchanging good practice, a concrete set of standards would now act as the new governing technology in the field of European education. From now on, the production of statistical reports by Member States would double. New categories of educational structures were being invented, such as participation in compulsory schooling or learning-to-learn. A different European education space was in the making; it would be governed by numbers and quality standards.

According to Dale (2006, pp. 36-38) and Rinne (2007), the OMC aims to establish guidelines for the EU, combined with specific timetables for achieving the Lisbon goals, through quantitative and qualitative indicators and benchmarks that assess the EU member states against the best in the world and through coordination and comparison to translate these European guidelines into national and regional educational policies. Furthermore, the OMC supports constant comparison through periodic monitoring, evaluation and peer review as mutual learning processes. In all of these processes a key element is the visibility of performance (Walters & Haahr, 2005, pp. 125-128). Visibility brings the possibility of peer pressure. Visibility requires indicators and data sets that are legible and public.

Apart from statistics, the OMC became the stimulus for other initiatives in the creation of the basis for the measurement and comparison of the European education systems. One of these first initiatives was to set up nine working groups of national experts and a 'Standing Group on Indicators and Benchmarks'. Information exchange, study visits and shared ideas of good practice would guide the work of the groups for the next three years (European Commission, 2003a). Although networks of professionals were the main agents of cooperation before, it was the first time that committees of experts from the Member States had officially been given the task of devising common standards for all European education systems. This 'magistracy of influence' (Lawn & Lingard, 2002) consisted of people who would work solely on furthering the European dimension of education, ensure high quality and relevance and improve the effectiveness of education and training in Europe. In some ways, the problems of harmonization and subsidiarity were now to be faced not only by Commission officials but mainly by representatives from the Member States themselves.

The initial work programme of 2002 comprised of a list of 33 indicators, which was reduced by the Standing Group on Indicators and Benchmarks to a list of 29. Some of the indicators related to the age of teachers; the ratio of pupils to teaching staff; the rate of completion of upper secondary education; improvement of attainment for low-performing students in reading literacy; performance in reading, maths and science; public expenditure on education; and participation in lifelong learning.

Apart from indicators relating to performance measurement, the 2002 work programme set also reference criteria (benchmarks) for the education systems across Europe. Even though two benchmarks had already been set in Lisbon, the Commission, through its communication in November 2002, suggested five benchmarks for European education (European Commission, 2002c):

- Member States should at least halve the rate of early school leavers, with reference to the rate recorded in the year 2000, in order to achieve an EU average rate of 10% or less.
- Member States should at least halve the level of gender imbalance among graduates in mathematics, science and technology whilst

securing an overall significant increase in the total number of graduates, compared to the year 2000.

- Member States should ensure that the average percentage of 25-64-year-olds in the EU with at least upper secondary education reaches 80% or more.
- The percentage of low-achieving 15-year-olds in reading, mathematical and scientific literacy should be at least halved in each Member State.
- The EU average level of participation in lifelong learning should be at least 15% of the adult working-age population (25-64 age group) and in no country should it be lower than 10%.

The Commission's recommendations were discussed by the Education Council in May 2003, and a list of five benchmarks for European education to be achieved by 2010 was finally agreed:

- an EU average of no more than 10% of early school leavers;
- an increase of at least 15% in graduates in maths, science and technology and a decrease in gender imbalance;
- a completion rate of upper secondary education of at least 85% of 22-year-olds;
- a decrease of at least 20% on the year 2000 in the percentage of low-achieving 15-year-olds in reading literacy;
- an EU level of participation in lifelong learning of at least 12.5% of the adult working-age population (25-64 age group).

Point 26 from the Lisbon presidency conclusions had suggested a substantial increase in human resources investment, a benchmark that was repeated by the Commission recommendation; however, this was not taken up by the Education Council. Instead, it 'merely mentioned that investment in education and training is a long-term investment, which has positive effects on social cohesion and sustainable growth' (European Commission, 2006a, p. 217).

The 'Education and Training 2010' work programme was adopted jointly by the European Council and the European Commission in February 2002; since then, the expression 'Education and Training 2010' has been used to refer to the whole process of implementing the Lisbon objectives. A month later, in Barcelona, the heads of states or governments approved the work programme and committed themselves to the new European vision for the education systems of the Member States: they set out to make education a 'world quality reference' by 2010.

Nevertheless, due to the acceleration of Asian economies (mainly China and India), in combination with the enlargement of the European Union in 2004 and the ever-dominant pressures for securing social cohesion and promoting European citizenship, the objectives set in 2002 became harder and harder to achieve. A first review of the progress towards the agenda of 'Education and Training 2010' was delivered by the Commission in 2003 (European Commission, 2003b). The report was to be subsequently redrafted as a joint report of the Commission and the European Council. It was finally submitted to the spring European Council in 2004. The report emphasized the urgency of the need to implement the Lisbon goals and stressed that data was presenting an alarming picture in regard to a number of indicators for European education systems. For example, the rates of early school leavers were still relatively high; too many young people did not have an adequate literacy level; there was a shortage of qualified teachers and trainers in some countries; and investment in education still lagged a long way behind that of the United States, where 'the involvement of the private sector is five times higher than in the EU' (European Commission, 2003b). In order to set developments back on course for 2010, the Commission proposed to concentrate reforms and investment towards the goals of the knowledge-driven society. It suggested that professional development for teachers and trainers should be increased, and stressed the significance of establishing 'a Europe of education and training' through the setting of a European qualifications and competences framework (European Commission, 2003b).

The Commission Communication from 2003 set the tone for the next year's (2004) joint interim report by the European Council and the European Commission in relation to the Lisbon goals. This Communication was initially adopted by the Education Council in February 2004 and subsequently submitted at the next Brussels spring European Council meeting in March 2004 (European Council, 2004a). The Communication discussed the frequent discrepancy between the EU indicators and the slow reforms in national policies. In the report presented for the spring European Council, it stressed the need for the Member States to 'commit more firmly to pursuing the reforms defined since the Lisbon European Council' (European Commission, 2004b).

The spring European Council in Brussels (2004), in order to deal with what was beginning to seem to be an increasingly worrying – if not failing – situation, set up a group of international experts, the 'Kok group' (named after Wim Kok, the former premier of Netherlands). The task for this group was to assist the European Commission in delivering the mid-term review of the Lisbon strategy in 2005. The 'Kok report' (Kok et al, 2004) emphasized the challenges of globalization and the ageing European population. It stressed that the achievements of Member States since 2000 had been very modest and that more and urgent reforms were necessary. In particular, in relation to the OMC, the Kok report claimed that its leniency had led to a loose understanding of the significance of the indicators and benchmarking set in Lisbon, and argued for peer pressure and the planning of national action programmes by 2005.

Therefore, in the light of this report, the Commission adopted a reformed strategy towards 'Education and Training 2010'. Instead of the broader objectives set in 2002, the focus returned once again to stricter growth and employment objectives. In the Staff Working Paper of 2004 (European Commission, 2004a), new indicators were identified, with a focus on:

- Key competencies, and particularly learning-to-learn;
- Investment efficiency;
- Information and Communications Technology (ICT);
- Mobility;
- Adult education;
- Vocational education and training;
- Languages (requested by the Barcelona European Council? in 2002);
- Professional development of teachers and trainers; and
- Social inclusion and active citizenship.

Indeed, these indicators were submitted to the European Council in 2005 and were approved as the new strategy towards an effective implementation of the benchmarks for 2010. In the European Commission's communication to the spring European Council, apart from the macro- and micro-economic 'integrated' – as they were called – guidelines, the Commission proposes, according to Guidelines no. 23 and 24, to:

Expand and improve investment in human capital, through:
– inclusive education and training policies and action to facilitate significantly access to initial vocational, secondary and higher education, including apprenticeships and entrepreneurship training;
– significantly reducing the number of early school leavers;
– efficient lifelong learning strategies open to all in schools, businesses, public authorities and households according to European agreements, including appropriate incentives and cost-sharing mechanisms, with a view to enhancing participation in continuous and workplace training throughout the life cycle, especially for the low-skilled and older workers.

Adapt education and training systems in response to new competence requirements, by:
– raising and ensuring the attractiveness, openness and quality standards of education and training, broadening the supply of education and training opportunities and ensuring flexible learning pathways, and enlarging possibilities for mobility for students and trainees;
– easing and diversifying access for all to education and training and to knowledge by means of working time

organisation, family support services, vocational guidance and, if appropriate, new forms of cost-sharing;
– responding to new occupational needs, key competences and future skill requirements by improving the definition and transparency of qualifications, their effective recognition and the validation of non-formal and informal learning. (European Commission, 2005a, pp. 33-34)

Thus, in June 2005, the European Council adopted a much closer focus on education in relation to employment. According to the Kok report's recommendations, a *simplified* version of the OMC was required from now on from Member States; they were asked to produce single annual reports on the delivery of the reforms in their countries, now known as 'Lisbon National Reform Programmes for Growth and Jobs 2005-08' (European Commission, 2005c). A first assessment of the National Reform initiatives was delivered by the Commission's annual progress report on growth and jobs to the spring European Council (European Commission, 2006b).

Similarly, the Joint European Council/European Commission reports of 2006 and 2008 testified to some progress with the Lisbon objectives, but also significant lagging behind with the implementation of lifelong learning, the delivery of basic skills for all, the delivery of quality teacher training and investment in higher education, as well as transnational mobility (Council of the European Union, 2006, 2008). Finally, the 2009 Commission report, 'Key Competences for a Changing World', suggested that 'policy cooperation since 2002' had contributed to improvements in European education systems and announced that 'building on this approach, and fully respecting Member States' responsibility for their education systems, the Council endorsed a Strategic Framework for European Cooperation in Education and Training (ET 2020) in May 2009' (Council of the European Union, 2009, p. 2). The focus on this report was on the progress of eight key competences (according to the 2006 recommendation); (1) Communication in the mother tongue; (2) Communication in foreign languages; (3) Mathematical competence and basic competences in science and technology; (4) Digital competence; (5) Learning to learn; (6) Social and civic competences; (7) Sense of initiative and entrepreneurship; and (8) Cultural awareness and expression.

At a first glance, one could argue for a double retreat from the project of the convergence of compulsory schooling in European education. First, the OMC was to be left aside in the face of the need for urgent reforms which it was apparently too 'soft' to deliver. In addition, as in the pre-Lisbon era, vocational training and lifelong learning were to receive greater emphasis than schooling. The indicators which continued to carry equal weight were those more closely related to employment outcomes. Such a simplified and more focused approach might mean that some indicators have been silenced in this last report; however, the project of convergence seems to have become much tighter for the remaining ones.

Comparable data regarding the education systems in Europe continues to be gathered in ways that often reflect the shifts of discourses and governing processes described above. The next section examines three major reports which reflect the continuing and changing face of measuring quality assurance, namely the 'Key Data on Education in Europe' (2000, 2002, 2005), all published by Eurydice.

'Key Data on Education in Europe'

An Overview of the Eurydice Reports of 2000, 2002 and 2005

This section provides an overview of three reports on the 'Key Data on Education in Europe', published by Eurydice, Eurostat and the European Commission. It attempts to make some comparisons between the three reports and to show how indicators of the quality of the European education system changed over the period 2000-2005.

> The quality of education and lifelong learning are at the heart
> of debate in the Community and constitute one of the
> priorities for action by the European Union on behalf of
> European citizens. At the outset of the third millennium,
> education and training are destined to become an essential
> investment for the future of societies and a key area of
> cooperation between European countries. The European
> Commission firmly believes that, if this cooperation is to be
> intensified and enriched, the availability of a basic set of
> different kinds of reliable, readily comparable indicators on
> education systems is an important requirement. (Eurydice,
> 2000, p. 1)

The 'Key Data' reports have been published by the Eurydice network since 1994. They are a valuable source of information regarding developments across the European education systems. The indicators measured are chosen by the Eurydice network and the Eurostat national partners. Both quantitative and qualitative information is gathered for the reports; Eurostat is in charge of the statistical information. The qualitative part comprises of descriptive indicators, a responsibility of Eurydice.

In particular, statistical data is gathered through what is called the UOE data collection: this is an established cooperation amongst UNESCO, OECD and Eurostat:

> The UOE data collection is an instrument through which these
> three organisations jointly collect internationally comparable

data on key aspects of educational systems on an annual basis
using administrative sources. (Eurydice, 2000, p. 26)

The data collected covers information regarding school enrolments,
school entrants, graduates and public expenditure, and includes level of
education, sex, age, type of curriculum, institution, field of study and
nationality. This was structured by educational level in accordance with
the UNESCO International Standard Classification for Education (ISCED
1997 [OECD, 1999]). An additional source of data for the 2000 report was
the European Union Labour Force Survey (LFS); carried out since 1983,
it provides annual reports on employment and unemployment statistics
in the EU. Regarding the 2005 report, findings from the PISA (2000 and
2003) and PIRLS [5] (2001) empirical surveys, carried out by OECD and
IEA respectively, were also used.

The 2000 Key Data report (Eurydice, 2000) groups indicators into 10
categories: Context; Structures and schools; Pre-primary education;
Primary education; Secondary education; Tertiary education; Teachers;
Special education; Foreign languages; and Information and
communications technology. In the 2002 report, the chapters on special
education and information and communications technology were
withdrawn, since data on these fields was produced in separate
publications, and a new chapter on the financing of education was
added.

However, it is in the 2005 report where most of the changes in
terms of the structure of the separate thematic categories of indicators
can be found. Thus, apart from giving data in relation to 'Context', the
rest of the indicators are grouped under the new sections 'Organisation',
'Participation', 'Resources', 'Educational processes' and 'Graduates and
qualification levels'. Indeed, new indicator groupings appear in this
report in the format of sub-sections; hence, 'Organisation' is now
examined not only through looking at 'Structures' (as in the reports of
2000 and 2002), but also examines 'Objectives and evaluation', as well as
'Decision-making levels and processes. For example:

'Objectives and evaluation'

- Over half of all European countries identify skills that children
  should possess on completion of pre-primary education;
- The evaluation of schools providing compulsory education is very
  widespread;
- Internal evaluation is sometimes based on the standard criteria of
  external evaluation;
- The findings of internal evaluation are generally used to carry out
  external evaluation;
- Publication of school evaluation practice is not common practice;
- Pupil assessment data are often used for school self-evaluation;

- A variety of information sources are used to monitor education systems;
- External tests designed specifically for monitoring the education system are becoming increasingly widespread.

Further, there is no division of the different school levels in the 2005 report, as there had been in the previous two reports. Therefore, instead of examining pre-primary, primary, secondary and tertiary education, the 2005 report looks at all stages under the general term 'Participation'. Hence, many of the previous indicators have either been moved to new categories, such as 'teaching time', 'grouping and assessment of pupils' (under the section 'Educational processes') or have disappeared completely. In terms of 'Resources', apart from examining the sub-section 'investment and equipment' and 'teachers', the new sub-section, 'management staff', has been added. Finally, in terms of 'Educational processes', new data on 'graduates and qualification levels' has been entered in this report.

In terms of further changes or absences, the number of indicators examining data in relation to teachers seems to have doubled over the course of two years: in the 2000 report, some of the findings relate to the duration and training of pre-primary teachers, the percentage of teachers working part-time, their retirement age or their minimum and maximum salaries. In terms of the 2002 report, emphasis is given to the teachers' professional training in university education, the ratio of pupils to teaching staff and the percentage of women teachers, whereas the indicator regarding teachers' salaries has been withdrawn. In the 2005 report, two new indicators have been added which relate to the frequency of teachers meeting and sharing information regarding materials and approaches. Also, under the sub-section 'management staff', indicators such as 'training of school heads in internal evaluation' have been added.

Examining the evolution of indicators and benchmarking in European education through the Eurydice, Eurostat and European Commission Key Data reports was a fairly brief and sketchy exercise, undertaken in order to gain a picture of the kinds of data on European education that have been officially considered worth collecting.

Conclusion

According to Anders Fogh Rasmussen, Prime Minister of Denmark, commenting on the Lisbon Strategy, 'the good thing is that all the symbolic elements are gone, and that which really matters – the core – is left' (Jyllands-Posten, 2000, quoted in Shore, 2000). As discussed above, all the European 'symbolic elements' were indeed gone for good after the Lisbon Strategy. It seems that 'the core' – quality and efficiency– is not merely to be found as the central component of European education policy in the post-Lisbon era; it is the core and the periphery, and everything education – or, to be accurate, lifelong learning– is about. Although the Euro-symbols of the 1980s, like the Erasmus programme and other constructs of the older European 'common culture' project, still hold strong, the language of numbers has gained an 'extraordinary' significance, as a top official from the Commission argued:

> And because of Lisbon ... the work on indicators exploded. I think I had one person or two, I had one person working on the indicators, that was the person that took care of all of this ... So we developed that slowly and I think that now, five, seven years later we have about, between 40 and 50 people working in the field. Inside the Commission ... . It is exploding. Extraordinary. (Interview with Commission official, March 2007)

For a long time in the history of the European education space, education governance was exercised through technologies of the 'self' (Foucault et al, 1988) which had systematically been working towards establishing new normative categories and constructing new meanings: these were notions such as the 'common European values', the 'common culture', or the notion of 'Europeanness'. According to Shore, 'constructing Europe requires the creation of "Europeans", not simply as an objectified category of EU passport holders and "citizens", but, more fundamentally, as a category of *subjectivity*' (2000, p. 30). The previous chapter has shown the modernist approaches taken in the construction of a European subjectivity, which, by often being astonishingly direct and almost propagandistic, were sometimes harshly criticized and rejected (Delanty, 1995). The old European myth was indeed a myth of high, elitist European culture, a myth of Enlightenment ideals commonly created and treasured by the European peoples – white middle- or upper-class men, in their majority. Nevertheless, these ideals had a strong social dimension which became particularly appealing and promising after the devastation and despair of the two world wars. The Member States of the European Union were invited into a project to build a social Europe which would establish itself as the significant 'Other' against the inhumanity of an economic system of winners and losers, which was accelerating to global dominance.

However, it soon turned out that the 'people's Europe' was not sufficient to respond to the demands of the new millennium. Despite subsidiarity, the field of education served for over three decades in the project of the creation of a European common identity. In history and geography, in narratives and tradition, Europe became a classical value – education and culture, through over-emphasizing commonalities and sidelining differences, were handy crutches in lifting the idea of Europeanization.

At the same time, national education systems remained more or less the same; they welcomed exchanges and networks as the additional European 'extra', which offered a fresher flavour of cosmopolitanism in their somewhat stale school curricula of the old Europe. Despite the systematic efforts to create a common European education space, education in the pre-Lisbon era remained largely a national topic. In the face of globalization and the dominance of the knowledge economy, new and urgent technologies of persuasion had to be devised; the voluntary nature of the previous arrangement was too loose to respond to the severe economic challenges of both the education and the wider market. Creating, regulating and monitoring, or in other words, governing the European education space now had to be based on statistics and what Rose calls 'governing by numbers' (1991). In fact, one of the greatest post-Lisbon developments in the history of the EU is the weight given to education and training in Europe; *first*, for the EU, rather than being an area at the periphery of policy making, education and learning have now become central in constructing Europe itself. Europe does not need to pre-exist in the hearts and minds as it was before – it is being created, sorted, systematized, scrutinized and constantly improved through the new soft governance tools of comparison and benchmarking. Hard EU regulation, in areas such as agriculture or trade for example, often meet the resistance and criticism of 'Euro-sceptics'; 'soft' law (Lawn, 2003), on the other hand, is self-imposed and self-adhered to – it is effective, manageable and economical, it looks optional and 'light-touch', it seems objective and forward-looking, and it relates to current concerns. *Second*, for the member-nations, in the field of education, Europe has become the relatively friendlier face of globalization: it gives them a platform to raise their voice; it offers them a quality assurance framework, many of which would otherwise have to devise it on their own; it often provides them with best practice advice, leaving the content of the curriculum intact; above all, it offers them a scapegoat, blaming which they can undisputedly justify the necessity for modernization and reform.

However, no matter how misguided 'Euro-romantics' have been, Rasmussen is also seriously wrong – the 'core' is not stripped of ideological and symbolic weight. The new technology of the governance of the European education space through indicators and benchmarks is not only to be seen as the project of fulfilling Brussels' requirements of achieving specific goals and objectives. Instead, it has to be examined as the deeply penetrating, consciousness-moulding and thus serious business of constructing new categories of (educational) thought and action – the project of re-inventing a 'new' European identity of competitive advantage and responsible individualism. According to Hacking, 'the bureaucracy of statistics imposes not just by creating administrative rulings but by determining classifications within which people must think of themselves and of the actions that are open to them'

(1991, p. 194). At their best these new governance technologies have offered a more coherent and organized framework for the improvement of the quality of education systems across Europe; at their worst, they are simply transforming education cultures and traditions, every aspect of teaching and learning, into tables and graphs, devoid of meaning, political context or any sense of history and place.

Above all, statistics do not convey much about the context in which data are interpreted; policy makers are too ready to find quick-fix solutions to problems which might need far closer scrutiny and understanding. Data prompt to fast action; understanding the context around them requires time and debates that neither can be afforded nor are desired. Above all, numbers have become an objective, irreversible 'truth'; context could only complicate or question it, hence it is unwelcome. According to a key European policy actor:

> The way the data are interpreted, the way they are used, the way we use them at EU level is crucial for the issue of the quality of the system because it can have a perverse effect if it is too narrow a perspective ... Quality and efficiency can really not be measured without having elements which are more reliable, based only on the figures that we have so far. But it is a political will to do it so the policy makers have to be more open and patient to qualitative information. My fear is that there is a tendency because of the pressure of time, because of the decisions that they have to make, that they finally decide on data which are largely insufficient or too narrow. Really too narrow, and we should not encourage that. (Interview with ex-Eurydice staff member, March 2007)

Lawn argues: 'Losing national reference points and a sense of national purpose or destiny while at the same time being situated in a raw state of marketization or commodification raises questions about how the EU can successfully invent a new identity with its own mission and purpose, developing and legitimating itself' (Lawn, 2003, p. 327). This chapter has attempted to show the significance of understanding that the shift to 'governing by numbers' is not merely a discursive, cosmetic or surface change, but in fact could be understood as the very process which has become one of the central components of building the new Europe of the knowledge economy. There seems to be a serious imbalance in the history of the construction of the European education space: from almost obsessively focusing on the 'big' history of a very remote past that belonged to few and was of interest to even fewer, Europe has turned to an almost anxiety to forecast, control and shape a one-way future. Investigating the rise of education data, with all their forms, processes, significant actors, national and international sites of production and policy analysts, means rendering visible the new ways of governing education. The European educational space is being constructed at the interface between states and EU offices, between offices and sub-contractors, academics and politicians, experts and officials, consultants and researchers. This space appears between European countries, in EU/state relations, in mentalities, in non-European agencies, and in a wide range of expert, managerial and professional actors in constant interaction with each other.

CHAPTER 7

The New Political Work
of Calculating Education

As we saw in the previous chapter, the shift towards a 'Europe of Knowledge' in the late 1990s involved an intensification of the early work on collaboration, networks and symbolic acts, and – above all – the systematization of the collection of education data. Data were important for overcoming the sensitivity towards national policies and planning and the obstacles to Europeanization they had been previously raising. Indeed, the rule of subsidiarity had a number of important effects: a lack of harmonisation of approaches and objectives, as well as the complete heterogeneity of education systems and numerous technical, administrative and regulatory barriers.

The management of combined economic and social policies (especially in the broad area of education and research) had a new strategy. Now, it would be focused on outputs and not on inputs (a cause of endless negotiations). It was to be based on information about systems and progress towards goals; the focus of action shifted from the constituent states to other social actors (cities, companies, public–private partnerships, research agencies, etc.) and onto the individual. It was argued that only 'the most sustained effort to education and training' would enable the development of a knowledge-based society. Education, in its new transparency as an area of goals and data about progress, and about systems and individual learning, would move from the shadows of culture and identity through the 'gradual construction of an open and dynamic European educational area' (European Commission, 1997, p. 3).

At the same time, the creation of an internal European identity was being overshadowed – even replaced – by the need to create an external global identity. The knowledge society or economy is present in many contemporary policy documents in Europe and beyond, and certainly within the policy frameworks of major international agencies, such as the World Bank and the OECD. It is not specific to the EU. International comparison as a means of achieving goals is part of the dominant form of governance within individual states in Europe, as they become sites of international capital flows and 'open business' environments.

As a result, the new EU outputs of education, as part of an integrated field of action (for example, with employment, economic growth and social exclusion), needed to have their data categories for collection and comparison restandardized. As an example of the new policy shift, a task force on lifelong learning and statistical data was created, which included:

> Representatives from different Directorates General (Education and Culture, Employment and Social Affairs, Research, EuroStat), from 5 Member States (Germany, Netherlands, Portugal, Finland, UK), from the European Centre for the Development of Vocational Training (CEDEFOP), the European Unit of the Eurydice network of Ministries of Education, the Advisory Committee on Statistics in the Economic and Social Spheres (CEIES), the Organisation for Economic Cooperation and Development (OECD) and the UNESCO Institute for Statistics (UIS), the International Labour Office (ILO) as well as two experts in the field from Denmark and Switzerland. (European Commission, 1997, p. 5)

In this way, the new strategy of building Europe, involving a redefined education at its core, had to be fabricated by experts drawn from international partners, a range of internal data agencies, and several Directorates General.

However, although learning became more and more fluid and networked, education has still been largely decided within closed national borders. In governing terms, this has been a fascinating paradox which in many ways has mobilized the research and thinking behind this book; it has mobilized it not only in terms of the questions it poses in regard to processes of European integration in an area where the dreaded 'h' word (harmonization!) has (still) to be avoided at all costs, but crucially because it has involved a large and growing number of education policy actors who have been trying – in very challenging, often frustrating and sometimes even comic situations – to work out some kind of coordination of objectives across Member States.

Therefore, this chapter focuses on, first, giving an overview of two of the organizations that have been crucial in making the European education data dream happen; and second, following two key actors (representatives, to an extent, of the kinds of data work that the organizations have delivered) as they narrate their experiences and views about trying to achieve consensus through data.

Constructing Data: European agencies

There are two key agencies involved in producing education data for the European Union – Eurostat and Eurydice. During recent years, Eurostat has increasingly worked with additional partners to extend and deepen the range of its educational statistics. Such significant partners have, for example, been the OECD and the IEA, and other international organizations (such as the United Nations, the International Monetary Fund and the World Bank). Statistics in education across Europe have not flowed through one agency, but, increasingly, they are managed by a coalition of agencies, particularly UNESCO, OECD and the EU (through Eurostat); the merging of their statistical work means that it is often difficult to separate them. Categories through which quantitative data are collected have had to be integrated and agreements had also to be reached about their scope and meaning – in other words, standards had to be agreed. As the EU has harmonized its data across different fields of work, accession and candidate countries, and through new intensive and detailed indicators, data management and distribution have become more important. There are several sources of comparative information which are increasingly combined and which depend on each other. Firstly, the necessary standardization tasks, necessary for comparison, were produced over time within Eurostat (for quantitative information) and by Eurydice (system comparative information and the European Education Thesaurus). Secondly, the categories or indicators alter over time as systems and areas for comparison alter (for policy reasons). Thirdly, categories or indicators become wider in scope and standardized internationally as they become used in global comparison (i.e. OECD, UNESCO and EuroStat collaborations and standards).

Eurostat

The Statistical Office of the European Communities (Eurostat) is tasked with providing a high-quality statistical information service at European level that enables comparisons between countries and regions, and which uses a common statistical 'language' (embracing concepts, methods, structures and technical standards) developed over time. Founded in 1953 to support the Coal and Steel Community, by 2009 Eurostat had around 900 staff, being a mixture of its own officials and seconded national experts, with the main task being to 'compare apples with apples':

> Eurostat does not collect data. This is done in Member States by their statistical authorities. They verify and analyse national data and send them to Eurostat. Eurostat's role is to consolidate the data and ensure they are comparable, using harmonized methodology. Eurostat is actually the only provider of statistics at European level and the data we issue are harmonized as far as possible.[6]

A significant event in the development of this service occurred in June 1997 when Article 212 was inserted into the Amsterdam Treaty, providing European Community statistics with a constitutional basis for the first time:

> the Council ... shall adopt measures for the production of statistics where necessary for the performance of the activities of the Community. (Treaty of Amsterdam, 1997, p. 47)

Previously, statistics were made available between members on the basis of agreement. So the European Statistical System (ESS) was built up gradually with the objective of providing comparable statistics at EU level. The ESS comprises Eurostat and the statistical offices, ministries, agencies and central banks that collect official statistics in EU Member States. It functions as a network in which Eurostat's role is to lead the way in the harmonization of statistics in close cooperation with the national statistical authorities. It then processes, analyses and publishes that data at a European level, following common statistical concepts, methods and standards. Eurostat defines common methodologies together with the Member States, consolidates the data collected in each country, ensures that it is harmonized and as comparable as possible, and then creates European aggregates for the 25 Member States. With the introduction of the European Monetary Union (EMU), Eurostat acquired greater significance as it is the main statistical agency which collects specific indicators related to the EMU area; since 1998 (the start of the EMU) Eurostat has been working with four-year statistical programmes, which are renewed in order to reflect new statistical and policy priorities – the latest one covers the period 2008-12. Eurostat publishes most of these data and analyses on its website, and in many cases also in the form of paper publications. In 2004, for the first time Eurostat began offering its data free of charge for research purposes. Despite the focus on the EMU and the EU-regulated policy areas, harmonization has been extended to nearly all statistical fields.

Throughout the late twentieth century, the development of projects for comparison, data collection and harmonization was being sustained by projects on cross-institutional collaboration, documentation and statistics, recognition of qualifications, and key organizations, like Eurostat, EuroBarometer or the European Education Thesaurus. First designed by UNESCO in the early 1970s, the International Standard Classification of Education (ISCED) was meant to serve 'as an instrument suitable for assembling, compiling and presenting statistics of education both within individual countries and internationally' (OECD, 1999). Since 1997, UNESCO, OECD and Eurostat have collaborated for the design of ISCED, in order to take into account changes in education and to anticipate future trends, and to enable common definitions and criteria for quality control to be used during the collection of the data in the different states. However, common definitions and categories may exclude past categories used in managing national educational systems, as they often need to discard them in order to move to common classifications which enable better international comparisons to be made. A central characteristic of international comparisons is an emphasis on recent performance due to the lack of comparable data over time. This collaboration between the OECD, Eurostat and UNESCO means that the problems of diverse international classification systems, necessary to judge competitiveness and improvement, are gradually being overcome in order for governing at a distance to be achieved.

The policy field of lifelong learning could be seen as an interesting example of the depth and width of harmonization, underpinned by statistical data. The ESS created a special task force on lifelong learning and statistical data (in 2001) to bring together all the current demands for numerical information and indicators from within European programmes, and those demanded by new intentions for social and economic development (European Commission, 2001a). As the EuroStat task force on lifelong learning pointed out:

> At the same time, responsibility for education and learning
> shifts from the public (state) to non-governmental
> organisations as well as to the individuals themselves ... .
> While traditional educational institutions have been (and still
> are) primarily concerned with transmitting knowledge,
> modern learning opportunities and the LLL [lifelong learning]
> approach put the emphasis on the development of individual
> capabilities and the capacity of the person to learn. At the
> heart of the LLL concept lies the idea of enabling and
> encouraging people 'to learn how to learn'. (European
> Commission/Eurostat, 2001)

Lifelong learning will reconstitute education, widening the field, integrating its functions, centring the individual learner, and stressing performance and comparing. Comparison will be easier after the landscape has been reordered and made transparent (European Commission, 2001a).

The integration of policy that was brought about through lifelong learning necessitated the integration of statistics not only from the education data collected by a range of international organizations and Eurostat itself but also of other relevant statistical data. For example, when producing annual education data reports, Eurostat sources go beyond the standard education data and include data drawn from demographic statistics, the Labour Force Survey (LFS), the 2000 LFS ad hoc module on transition from school to working life, the European Community Household Panel (ECHP), research and development statistics, health statistics and also economic statistics. This is a complex system of the harmonization of a multiplicity of data sources, necessary for the requirements of the new European data dream. In a sense, the new European project appears to be increasingly dependent on such data in order for the 'common objectives' to be achieved – the EMU in particular has intensified the need not only for data, but for the continuous monitoring of robust and transparent statistics, sometimes even imposed on Member States which do not obey the rules.

Eurydice

Eurydice is a cross-European institutional network for gathering, monitoring, processing and circulating reliable and readily comparable qualitative information on education systems and policies throughout Europe. The network is described as 'boosting' European cooperation in education by developing exchanges of information about systems and policies and producing studies on common issues. It works mainly for those involved in educational policy-making nationally and in the European Union institutions, as well as at regional and local levels. Within the ministries, information from Eurydice is intended primarily for ministerial secretariats and advisory staff; policy implementation staff; European and international relations divisions; research and forward planning departments; as well as senior European Commission staff responsible for devising and implementing educational policies and programmes.

Eurydice appears to be steered by regular contact with the Education Committee, which is constituted by representatives of the ministries of education and the European Commission; the Education Committee's main task is to prepare the business of the European Council and education ministers and to ensure that their decisions are implemented. Since its establishment in 1980, Eurydice has altered its foci to meet new policy directions; for example, since 2007 Eurydice has been included in the EU Action Programme in the field of Lifelong Learning, in which it helps to support the development of policies as well as collaboration at European level. It is cooperating with other partners in this area to mobilize all relevant expertise to produce an overall analysis of the area.

Its publications are divided into descriptions of national education systems, comparative studies devoted to specific topics, and indicators and statistics. First launched by the European Community, the Eurydice Network consists of a European coordinating unit in Brussels and 37 national units established by education ministries in 33 countries. The European unit coordinates the activity of the Network, drafts and distributes most of its publications, and designs and administers Eurydice databases and the central website. National units provide and are involved in processing the data on which this activity relies and ensure that the output of the Network reaches target groups within their countries. In most countries, units are situated within the education ministry or in resource and research centres.

Eurydice has been cooperating with Eurostat to update and regularly renew this broad spectrum of indicators since 1995, especially in the Key Data reports; it also cooperates with CEDEFOP. Since 2001, given the common objectives that education systems set themselves in the period up to 2010, the role and contribution of Eurydice has been seen as crucial. Eurydice's mission is to offer:

> Detailed descriptions and overviews of national education systems (National Education Systems and Policies);
> Comparative thematic studies devoted to specific topics of Community interest (Thematic Studies);
> Indicators and statistics (Key Data Series);
> A series of Facts and Figures related to education, such as national education structures, school calendars, comparison of salaries and of required taught time per countries and education levels (Facts and Figures).[7]

Eurydice produces system information, drawn from official sources, which it characterizes as a 'comparative education' approach:

> In drawing attention both to similarities and differences, comparative education aims to improve insight into the special features of systems and the interdependent relations between the factors that give rise to them. Its ultimate aim is to enlighten policy-making in the interests of better education.[8]

Its reports are described as a 'special kind of knowledge whose authority is based on academic principles', and which produce 'high quality reliable studies' [9] for policy makers and those responsible for the management and administration of education. Eurydice is viewed as an authoritative reference source as a result of its working methodology. All its comparative studies are subjected to this initial process, on which the validity of subsequent comparisons largely depends.

Constructing Europe: the role of actors

> Since the cooperation started in '76, the exchange of the information and the experiences between the member states has been the key instrument of cooperation because of subsidiarity – you can't regulate… . Since Lisbon the learning process between the member states has become a means to achieve the Lisbon strategy and not an end in itself. Before it was an end in itself, you do it because it was there, there was cooperation, you had teachers' networks, networks of policy

> makers and you make them exchange, you make them work on this exchange. Now there is a purpose. There are common objectives. Lisbon is the first time that ministers of education decided on common objectives. (Interview with European Commission staff member, March 2007)

This quotation signifies a marked change in how education policy in the European Union has been steered – from voluntary, informal and patchy to coordinated action towards the achievement of the Lisbon objectives. This is interesting and also important because it explains a marked change in the status, authority and work conditions of the specific actor who shared it with us working from a small office somewhere on the periphery of Brussels, with only five staff, at the beginning of the 2000s (when Martin Lawn first met him), by 2007 he was to be found at the top level of a magnificent glass tower in the centre of a city which itself had changed considerably – a city in the making, as was the project Europe.

> It changed much since that time (2000), yes, because at that time we had no data, and then we had some studies and we had Cedefop. And because of Lisbon ... the work on indicators exploded. I think I had one person or two, I had one person working on the indicators, that was the person that took care of all of this... There has been a lot of resistance in using indicators and statistics and we simply didn't have the competence in the house for doing it. So we developed that slowly and I think that now, five, seven years later we have about, between 40 and 50 people working in the field. Inside the Commission ... It is exploding. (Interview with European Commission staff member, March 2007)

Staff numbers increased as well as the responsibility for monitoring and reporting on the progress of the Member States towards the common goals; however, as suggested earlier with the case of Eurostat, indicator work could never be done in isolation. When data converges, work programmes need to harmonize too, and collaborations start to emerge; collaborations with global organizations that – for some at least – had a very different ideological basis on which they conducted research in education. Nonetheless, with a sharp increase in the budget and the need for data, such partnerships flourished:

> We invested also in a European survey on learning to learn skills which is a completely new instrument in development based on the bad experiences in PISA and TIMMS and then we support OECD and IEA in carrying out a number of surveys by supporting member states. We pay 80% of the national costs by the budget of the Union. So we have a budget for doing these things, I would believe around 20 million euros a

year, it is around that. (Interview with European Commission
staff member, March 2007)

These developments testify towards the establishment of a new era for
education policy making – the actual steering, and the governance of
European education systems from a centre. The increase of data and
indicators and their monitoring from Brussels suggests that comparisons
from now on would not be at the hands of the Member States. Data were
centrally collected and centrally reported – however, apart from
contributing to a graph, were they ever really used? Did they ever explain
anything? And why would the central actor know better that the national
one?

> *EC Officer*: Yes, we are overwhelmed with data and then we
> don't use them enough. We go to the next survey and then we
> have new data and so on. Well. I think there is a great
> difference between the data that countries need for monitoring
> the quality of their systems, like the English system which is
> monstrous. I always ask what is the cost–benefit. Have you
> ever made a cost–benefit analysis of what you are doing?
> *ML*: What is the answer?
> *EC Officer*: They smile.

He continues:

> [In] the Scottish system, everything is Scottish. This is our
> system, we defend it as a fortress and all these influences from
> outside, they should be kept away. By sitting here and making
> comparative analysis, you identify what is specifically
> Scottish to the Scottish system. What is it that you should
> actually defend to keep these roots in national culture and
> national institutions that are set up. We know it, or we could
> know it, we have the information, we have this distance that is
> necessary to do it. And we can compare and find out what is it
> that shines in the Scottish system (Interview with European
> Commission staff member, March 2007)

And he continues:

> I think what is the result of that knowledge is the value of
> diversity you find here. The understanding of the importance
> of diversity you find here. In national level you find some kind
> of backbone reaction to harmonisation. They are against it and
> we are the threat. But it is in this organisation, in this building,
> that you find people that know very well that the diversity is
> the ground for the efficiency of education, for the quality of
> education. You would not find anybody here that is for
> harmonization, they are the first to know that you cannot have

a European system of education, it does not exist, you could not invent it, it would not function ...

To identify the elements of success that are relevant to your country and which can be used in your country and have roots in your system, that's very very difficult and we don't have the methodology for doing it. But we can at least go from this logic of identifying objectively one way or another good performance and then approach an understanding of why and how they do that. Then at last inspire other countries to at least reflect what they can learn from that. (Interview with European Commission staff member, March 2007)

However, how are indicators really devised? And what is the role of such actors as those responsible for such work at the European Commission level? This is always a very interesting discussion, as the more one approaches the field and attempts to comprehend and explain it, the more tensions arise; the tensions are between robust data that need to inform evidence-based policy making and the political choices that have to be made in regard to what kinds of data should be collected; choices that are made after some hard negotiating has taken place:

I go to many of these [Ministers'] meetings. There are many formal speeches, interventions, prepared by their advisers. But then you put one agenda on the table and that is indicators. Then we ask the member states which are the indicators that you would use in measuring progress and quality of your education systems. Then civil war starts. These are the most passionate discussions we have in the Commission. And ministers are mobilised 100% and they are informed continuously about the discussion in the technical committee of the council, the education committee. But they have all, all the mantras from the ministry when they talk about these things. And they are all fighting like mad to get indicators that show their countries performing better. (Interview with European Commission staff member, March 2007)

This is not always as formal a process as research or policy might present it to be. Much of this 'political work' is done informally and a key actor who mediates the process has to be on top of it:

It happens in corridors, they talk together before, sure, somebody intervenes and others support ... Our work is to know beforehand what is happening. There are allies, get the arguments on the table. Negotiations have to happen. It is not just policy, it is content, knowledge about education systems. I find it fascinating. To work on indicators here is not statistical work. We need the statistical competence but it is political

work. Policy negotiations, what you can agree on, what you
want to look at when you want to measure quality of
education. (Interview with European Commission staff
member, March 2007)

Negotiations usually start from a very broad perspective in order to
consequently narrow the selection of indicators with a focus on current
policy priorities. These processes explain the changes that indicator
systems have gone through over the last decade; Europe has moved from
extensive lists to fewer and fewer indicators and to finally a single
indicator which was decided as one of the five (the other four reflecting
other policy areas) of the EU 2020 agenda. The following two quotations
could not be more eloquent in describing the slowness and arduousness
of the policy process:

> There was no willingness of identifying a European concept of
> quality of school education but there was a willingness of
> doing mechanical ... a technical exercise that you ask a simple
> question. A stupid question that you ask everybody, which
> indicators would you use for measuring quality in education.
> So we get all 150 indicators on the table. Nobody can agree on
> anything. But then we start agreeing on eliminating. And when
> you start eating that cake slowly, you end up with a limited
> number of indicators and you say these are the last ones that I
> would eliminate. This is how we ended up with 16 I think.
> (Interview with European Commission staff member, March
> 2007)

> There were a number of these 29 indicators that simply were
> bad and we knew it. So there was a need for what the council
> called the coherent framework. So they asked us to come back
> to the council and to report how we can identify a coherent
> framework. We had a long discussion with the member states
> – what is a coherent framework – and they answered the
> question you put in fact – what is a coherent framework that
> you would use in monitoring the progress of the Lisbon
> process in the field of education? We started with models of
> indicators, all statistical analysis, correlations between
> statistics that exist already. How could we identify an
> optimum tool? What we ended up with was a tool that was
> purely political, saying that a framework is a list of indicators
> of the policy issues that are on the table. (Interview with
> European Commission staff member, March 2007)

The choice of indicators reflects the growing significance of a policy
area, like lifelong learning for example – for some already a policy in

place, whereas for others still an 'exotic' concept – an idea that is not rooted in common practices and thus is fought against:

> We came with a suggestion of 20 indicators and they jumped immediately on those that were most sensitive and said, listen we don't want them. And these are as we called them the exotic indicators. They had problems with them. And they took them – these were the indicators on the multipurpose use of schools which is for example, you know in France, they close the school in the afternoon and it is not used for anything else – it is empty until the next morning. In Scandinavia they are open until midnight, used for adult education. All these which are structural developments are decided by the ministries in the countries. Schools can be used as local learning centres. We see that as a major step towards lifelong learning. So we wanted this indicator to find the data whether laws permit schools to do that – that was taken out immediately. (Interview with European Commission staff member, March 2007)

Once indicators have been decided, new contestations arise; those around comparison and the presentation of the results. The role of European Commission actors has been key here in order to completely overturn past European Commission practices in favour of more 'modern' and extrovert presentation of the 'results': from being extremely careful and politically aware of what problems a 'bad' result would have for those performers to following other international organizations' practice (like the OECD) for increasing peer pressure – the practice of naming and shaming:

> Very often for school education we go to the new member states. Slovakia is performing perfectly in secondary education, very very high levels. We identify these countries. High performers. Normally we identify the three best performers because this is what the ministers ask for. We also identify the worst performers but we can't say anything. So we identify the three best performers. The logic of it is that by identifying that we ask the question why – what is happening in these countries? They are just cheating with the statistics or have they taken specific decisions at the national level that make them perform well and is it possible to learn from them? (Interview with European Commission staff member, March 2007)

> It was decided in 2005 by Barroso to marginalize structural indicators because he didn't want to name and blame countries. I am saying that if he doesn't want to name and

blame countries the European Commission is a weak
Commission ... this area will only survive if you manage to
find a balance between naming and blaming and giving
comparative information about performance levels. It is all a
question of presentation. It is a question of policy.
(Interview with European Commission staff member, March
2007)

Nevertheless, how would the indicator story be told if someone were
working from a different research organization, that was expert in
collecting qualitative rather than statistical information? The second key
actor whose experience and views inform this analysis comes from
Eurydice. According to her, the development of lifelong learning and the
knowledge society in Europe instigated the drawing up and collection of
indicators and benchmarking before Lisbon – rather than the beginning,
Lisbon was the culmination of a process which had started earlier:

> The indicators work started before Lisbon. It started in 1995.
> Then the quality indicators, the indicators on lifelong learning
> in '96-'97; so there was, without knowing that Lisbon will
> come, there they were because of the lifelong learning
> development and the knowledge society which was not Lisbon
> in itself, it was before. So there was already development, not
> as open and as clear as in the Lisbon strategy but I would say
> that we live in a world where more and more, even in
> countries which were not so keen on that, measurement is
> important. So the efficiency of the public service is becoming a
> key dimension in the work. (Interview with ex-Eurydice staff
> member, March 2007)

Therefore, in what ways does a qualitative research organization cope
with the demand for more and more statistical data? Despite the fact that
statistics and measurement have acquired a central place in the new
governance of European education systems, qualitative and contextual
data are still necessary – firstly, because indicators are mostly descriptive
wordings of a policy priority and a common objective; and secondly,
because the only way to explain the reasons that some countries perform
better than others is to examine the political, cultural, and institutional
specificities of the context. Nevertheless, numbers still prevail:

> So in a way yes, the data, therefore indicators, have become a
> crucial dimension. If you have a political objective which is
> efficiency and performance, qualitative data is interesting yes,
> but if you don't have the quantitative data, you can't go back to
> the parliament and say well, this is where we are, but I don't
> know, I don't know how many. The return on investment is an
> ongoing process. In quite many countries they have to

113

> reinforce their statistical instruments in all sectors, which as I said was less developed over the past 10 years. So Lisbon is maybe making that phenomenon more acute, more important but I will not say that Lisbon is the origin of it. If you look at the Lisbon strategy, the conclusions of the head of states of March 2001, it is very much qualitative. Of course they say that indicators and benchmarks are tools for achieving competitiveness .... . But there are quite a lot of elements in the Lisbon strategy which still deal with societal problems. (Interview with ex-Eurydice staff member, March 2007)

The future of research organizations like Eurydice is in following the current policy priorities as well as establishing partnerships with other experts and researchers. In the end, the 'data dream' requires more than the setting of indicators and benchmarks:

> If you look at the five benchmarks which ministers of education have approved in 2003 it is very much surprisingly school-oriented – school, subsidiarity, not much higher education. You have school failure, literacy, what else, lifelong learning, participation, maths and science, so ... But you can't follow policy developments only through that prism of these five benchmarks. So I think that the future will very much depend on the capacity of the Commission using tools like Eurydice and Cedefop because you can't speak about lifelong learning and only deal with basic education, you have to have more joint work in order to catch the lifelong learning spectrum. (Interview with ex-Eurydice staff member, March 2007)

Concluding Comments

As with researching a continuously expanding policy field, the project of setting indicators and benchmarks for European education is a work in progress. This chapter has described some of the developments over the last decade towards establishing common frameworks for measuring and coordinating the European space of education. A number of issues emerged from this exercise.

First, indicators and benchmarks do not have a fixed identity; they are also not static in terms of content; particularly in the post-Lisbon era, we observe a constant reworking, redrafting, sometimes elaborating and often reducing work on indicators and always in relation to the most pertinent political and economic issues that the EU has been dealing with.

Nevertheless, if there is a tendency to constantly change education indicators according to dominant trends or political issues, the crucial question remains the same: which is the basis on which comparisons are made? Comparisons seem to work on examining educational systems alongside and at the present; nevertheless, can comparisons be established with categories of the past? In other words, are we experiencing a slow shift from comparing quantitative data to examine its findings through time, in using it to compare data mainly through (the European education) space? What are the implications of this?

Further, education in Europe appears as also less and less static than ever before. Rather, it is seen as an active process; as we have also identified earlier in the book, structures, such as buildings and classes, or traditional categories such as teachers' salaries, are withdrawn and new categories arise: teachers' teamwork or their part-time contributions. Even the traditional categories of examining educational systems through distinguishing between levels of education have been removed; the new overall indicator is 'participation'. However, participation is a term which has traditionally been used in lifelong learning discourses which connect education with other policy areas, and especially the labour market. However, what are the implications of integrating education indicators with those of employment and growth? Finally, if the project of setting indicators and benchmarks is indeed in constant flux and change, what is the future of education systems in the way we know them?

CHAPTER 8

The OECD as an Agent of Europeanization in Education: the impact of international education assessment tools

Introduction

As we have already seen, the European policy space in education is being created in several ways and – especially in recent years – through the production of data. However, it is important to recognize that the European Union is an agent as well as a conduit of Europeanization; it is an actor in a new policy area that is also populated by other international organizations and agencies. Indeed, one of the most powerful of institutional actors in the momentum for Europeanization is not a European agency but a global one, the OECD. As data has become crucial to governing, the growing expertise and policy influence of the OECD has changed its relation to the European Commission.

In this chapter, we focus on an analysis of the OECD as a significant actor in the governance of the European education space and suggest that, through its impact on national education systems in Europe, although apparently separate and distinct, the OECD plays a rather indirect, but no less important role on the governance of the European education space. An example of this kind of influence and role is the OECD Programme for International Student Assessment (PISA), which although a global phenomenon, nevertheless has had an enormous impact not only on reforms of European education systems but crucially in establishing a new kind of 'measuring' logic about governing education in Europe. In any case, Europe represents a substantial part of the OECD world; according to a key actor at the Education Directorate of the European Commission:

> We used to have great competition between the two
> institutions [OECD and the European Commission] which was
> that they were research-based, we were policy-based. And we
> needed that. They needed the policy aspect to mobilise the

> European consciousness ... it was in their interest working with us ... We had some differences but we are working closer and closer together, we are very very good friends now, there is no conflict. (Interview with Commission staff member, June 2009)

The chapter examines the role of the OECD in framing and steering education policy at a European and global level and moves on to briefly examine the first cycle of the PISA assessment (2000-2009). It uses three examples, the cases of Finland, Germany and the United Kingdom, and their responses to the PISA 2000 and 2003 assessments, in order to examine the ways in which PISA enters these national policy spaces and acts on them in ways that govern and shape education activity. The chapter then draws on interview data from key policy actors in Brussels to make a case for the significance and impact of such governing tools, not just at the national level, but also on other international organizations and their agencies, such as the European Commission. We conclude by suggesting that, as the policy officer above clearly argues, since the two international organizations have been sharing a broadly similar policy agenda for some time now, PISA and its effects may be seen as a useful tool in the project of building the new European education space of competitiveness and cohesion (Council of the European Union, 2000a).

OECD and the Politics of Comparison

Alongside other international organizations, the OECD has become part and parcel of the internationalizing, globalizing and thus converging policy processes that have been commented on by many scholars in relation to education (Taylor et al, 1997; Ozga & Lingard, 2007). While it is primarily concerned with economic policy, education has taken on increasing importance within that mandate, as it has been reframed as central to national economic competitiveness within an economistic human capital framework and linked to an emerging 'knowledge economy'. Founded in 1961, the OECD has taken on an enhanced role as a policy actor, as it seeks a niche in the post-Cold-War globalizing world in relation to other international organizations and supranational agencies (Henry et al, 2001; Rinne et al, 2004). To this end, it has developed alliances with other international organizations such as UNESCO, the European Union, and the World Bank to actively promote its policy preferences. The case of the OECD is particularly interesting because, unlike the EU, it does not have the legal instruments or the financial levers to actively promote policy making at the national level within member nations. This also contrasts with the World Bank, for example, which has 'power' over nations of the Global South through policy requirements or trade-offs (structural adjustment) linked to funding and loans. Nonetheless, through ranking exercises such as the 'Education at a Glance' annual reports, the International Adult Literacy Survey (IALS), its Indicators in Education project, including the World Education Indicators developed in conjunction with UNESCO and the World Bank, through PISA and through national and thematic policy reviews, its educational agenda has become significant in framing policy options not only at the national but also in the constitution of a global policy space in education (Lingard et al, 2005; Lingard & Grek, 2007).

Responses to the increased significance globally of education/ learning as a policy area have tended to focus on the top-down policy influence of international organizations and the transfer of policy from the international to the national level (see, for example, Taylor et al, 1997; Ball, 1998). However, to date, there has been little attention to education policy learning at the *transnational* level, especially within Europe. Current research (Grek et al, 2009a) suggests that European Commission and OECD education policies are received at the national level as relatively homogeneous, and this prompts questions about their relationship in terms of policy direction over recent years, and especially since the Lisbon Strategy in 2000. Following the emphasis in the Kok Report (Kok et al, 2004) on global, free market, rather than European-based education policies and programmes (Robertson, 2007), as well as the increased significance of the skills and competences policy agenda (Grek, 2009, 2010), we focus on an enquiry into the nature and direction of policy learning between international organizations, through the examination of international comparative studies as tools in governing education in Europe.

While research in this area is limited (but see Finnemore, 1993; Stone, 2004; Porter & Webb, 2004), the key consideration is that international organizations are not 'mere epiphenomena' of an impersonal policy machinery (Barnett & Finnemore, 1999) but purposive actors who, 'armed with a notion of progress, an idea of how to create a better life, and some understanding of the conversion process', have become the 'missionaries of our time' (Barnett & Finnemore, 1999, p. 712). For example, the OECD's transformation into a powerful agent of transnational education governance follows from the comparative turn towards 'a scientific approach to political decision making', that builds on data collection and the ranking and rating of member countries (Martens, 2007, p. 42). This approach highlights not only the significance of the OECD as an education policy agent, but crucially, the emergence of a social *matrix* of interrelated governing actors, who classify and construct meaning and articulate and diffuse new norms and principles.

Further, Power (1999; 2003a, b, 2004) and Strathern (2000, 2004) suggest that a 'metrological mood' (Power, 2004, p. 766) has become the mechanism through which education systems are measured and made accountable, and has permeated the structure and public face of international organizations themselves. A related, parallel development is the relatively recent 'evidence-based' or 'evidence-informed' policy-making trend, which builds on the assumption that as more evidence underpins policy, so it will become better and more rational (Davies et al, 2000; Davies, 2004; Nutley et al, 2002; Schuller & Burns 2007).

On the other hand, and as a parallel development at a European level, we observe a stark change in the European Commission's education policy-making tools, especially since 2000 and the Lisbon Strategy, which heralded increased emphasis on indicators and benchmarking, that were meant to drive change and push forward the agenda for growth and jobs. These new policy tools work as governing devices that, through the mutual learning of the policy makers and experts who come together for their development, their negotiations and co-options, together with cross-comparison and competition, draw national systems closer into European and global frameworks and practices. Similarly, although for much longer, the OECD has been cultivating and promoting technical expertise in creating comparable data sets (like PISA), where countries can potentially measure the success of their education systems against others and shift their policy orientations accordingly. In this new context, notions such as lifelong learning and the knowledge economy have turned education departments in both the European Commission and the OECD into central governing hubs. Thus, the development of new policy technologies, combined with the new significance of education redefined as (lifelong) learning, have together greatly enhanced the OECD's and European Community's governing capacity, not only in their use of monitoring and measuring, but crucially in their promotion of particular attitudes and dispositions to learning.

As a result, and drawing on Martens's (2007) ideas, we observe a taken-for grantedness about education indicators, despite all the commentary asking for contextualization in their interpretation (e.g. Nóvoa & Yariv-Mashal, 2003), and this is indicative of the way in which they have become an accepted part of the contemporary educational policy lexicon across the globe, within and well beyond the OECD, and of their growing significance to the work of the OECD itself since the 1980s. PISA now accounts for approximately 30% of the Education Directorate's budget inside the OECD and is funded directly by participating nations. One could suggest that the OECD's greatest impact has been in relation to its Indicators agenda, including PISA, and its role in constructing a global educational policy field through *governance by comparison* (Martens, 2007). Indeed, as Antonio Nóvoa argued, 'comparing must not be seen as a method, but as a policy ... the expert discourse builds its proposals through "comparative" strategies that tend to impose "naturally" similar answers in the different national settings' (Nóvoa & Lawn, 2002, p. 144).

Therefore, in its role as policy actor, the OECD has created a niche as a technically highly competent agency for the development of educational indicators and comparative educational performance measures. OECD-defined and collected data on education systems in Europe are then intersected with EU data, contributing to the creation of a governable space of comparison and commensurability – the European education space (Nóvoa & Lawn, 2002). Indeed, a number of histories of statistics demonstrate the intimate and interwoven relationships between the development of state administrative structures and processes of standardization and comparison (Hacking, 1975, 1990; Porter, 1995; Desrosières, 1998). The nation constituted as a 'space of equivalence' is necessary to the construction of statistics (Desrosières, 1998), but statistics and numbers which elide the local are equally important to the construction, in this case, of a commensurable education policy field. These developments reflect policy convergence around what Brown and his colleagues define as a new educational policy consensus:

> The new consensus is based on the idea that as the 'walled' economies in mid-century have given way to an increasingly global economy, the power of national government to control the outcome of economic competition has been weakened ... Indeed the competitive advantage of nations is frequently redefined in terms of the quality of national education and training systems judged according to international standards. (Brown et al, 1997, pp. 7-8)

The education work of the OECD has become a very important node in this complex policy field, as education policy is seen as central to the competitive advantage of national economies in the face of globalization. Evaluations of national education and training systems require international points of comparison. The OECD has filled this niche in relation to education policy in terms of its work on indicators generally and specifically through PISA. Taken together, these factors account for the increased significance of the education work of the OECD, its contribution to the emergent global education policy field, and its enhanced role as policy actor. In the next section we look in more detail at the organization and content of PISA.

The Programme for International Student Assessment

The Programme for International Student Assessment (PISA) is conducted in three-yearly cycles and examines the knowledge and skills of 15-year-olds in compulsory education. The OECD develops the assessment tasks used in PISA through commissioning agencies to produce the tests. Thus, PISA works with tests that are developed and mandated by OECD. Although PISA began as a joint study of the OECD member countries, it has developed its scope to involve non-member countries as well. Indeed, since the year 2000, when the first PISA study was conducted, more and more countries have been taking part, with the latest PISA (2009) having assessed students in 67 countries all over the world, thus involving almost 90% of the world's economy. This shows the significance given to the tests globally, since even countries which are not OECD members want to be seen to be taking part in the international comparison. According to a policy actor in England asked about the participation of non-member states in PISA, these countries:

> might choose to see PISA as more relevant for them or
> certainly in terms of the comparisons you can make. They
> don't necessarily want to be making comparisons with
> countries like them, they often want to be making comparisons
> with the member countries and the economic part, how far
> they have got to go in order to catch up ... They come to PISA
> because they want to be compared with these leading
> countries. (Interview with English policy actor, 2007)

This international dimension of the survey, which overrides the boundaries of Europe to compare student performance in countries as diverse as the United States, Greece and Indonesia, gives PISA a particularly significant weight as an indicator of the success or failure of education policy. PISA is the OECD's platform for policy construction, mediation and diffusion at a national, international and, possibly, global level (Rizvi & Lingard, 2006).

Instead of evaluating knowledge on the basis of the curriculum or the cultural and life experiences that 15-year-olds have, PISA:

> provides international comparisons of the performance of
> education systems, with strong, cross-culturally valid
> measures of competencies that are relevant to everyday, adult
> life. Assessments that test only mastery of the school
> curriculum can offer a measure of the *internal* efficiency of
> school systems. They do not reveal how effectively schools
> prepare students for life after they have completed their formal
> education. (OECD, 2001, p. 27)

The concepts of comparison and internationalization give PISA its substance, since it is in the comparisons of school outcomes across the world that policy makers can now find answers to their problems:

> PISA offers a new approach to considering school outcomes,
> using as its evidence base the experiences of students across
> the world, rather than in the specific cultural context of a
> single country. The international context allows policy-makers
> to question assumptions about the quality of their own
> country's educational outcomes. (OECD, 2001, p. 27)

Decontextualization, commensurability and policy orientation have been the key ingredients contributing to PISA's success. However, the sheer scale of the enterprise may distract attention from fundamental questions about its purposes and effects. For example, one should not lose sight of the importance of PISA as a 'shop front' for OECD. Through advertising the OECD's capacity to do such work, it has become the evaluator of choice. The assessment of comparative system performance has direct effects on the shaping of future policy directions, and the reporting of PISA results adds to the sense of urgency in responses to PISA, as Nóvoa and Yariv-Mashal point out:

> Such researches produce a set of conclusions, definitions of 'good' or 'bad' educational systems, and required solutions. Moreover, the mass media are keen to diffuse the results of these studies, in such a manner that reinforces a need for urgent decisions, following lines of action that seem undisputed and uncontested, largely due to the fact that they have been internationally asserted. (Nóvoa & Yariv-Mashal, 2003, p. 425)

PISA has been conducted four times to date: in 2000, 2003, 2006 and 2009. While always testing reading, mathematical and scientific literacy, its innovative dimension – and part of its interest as a governing device – lies in the fact that, as noted above, it does not examine students' mastery of school curricula; rather the focus is on an assessment of young people's ability to practically apply their skills in everyday life situations. The focus on 'real-life' circumstances and on students' capacity to enter the labour market with core skills, such as literacy and numeracy, has taken PISA's focus of interest away from less explicit educational aims that resist measurement (e.g. democratic participation, artistic talents, understanding of politics, history, etc.), towards a more pragmatic view of education's worth: 'its relevance to lifelong learning' (OECD, 2003), Indeed, PISA is one of the first international student assessment surveys that applies concepts such as 'literacy', previously connected only with adult learners, to school pupils. According to OECD, PISA has an:

> innovative approach to lifelong learning, which does not limit PISA to assessing students' curricular and cross-curricular competencies but also asks them to report on their own motivation to learn, their beliefs about themselves and their learning strategies. (OECD, 2003, n.p.)

This is significant, since lifelong learning is seen to expand and include compulsory education. This emphasis on lifelong learning is indicative of the concern to embed responsibility for continuous self-improvement and upskilling in the individual learner from a relatively early stage in their development. It connects the production of data to the growing self-governance of active subjects, and extends governance into a system of self-regulation (Rose, 1992; Ball, 1998). Finally, and perhaps most significantly, according to the same document, a key feature of PISA is: 'its policy orientation, with design and reporting methods determined by the need of governments to draw policy lessons'.

Hence, it is made clear that this is not simply a testing regime – it is constructed and operates under a clear and specific policy framework, which is to be adopted by the participant countries if they are to improve their future PISA assessments and thus improve their standing in attracting economic and human capital investment.

PISA has come a long way in a short period of time and has consolidated the role of the OECD and its Education Directorate as the pre-eminent global organization for developing and analysing comparative international educational performance data. PISA results now receive a very high profile within national media and are present in the consciousness of senior policy makers. Media coverage of PISA results is very substantial and perhaps represents another manifestation of the 'mediatization' of education policy processes (Fairclough, 2000; Lingard & Rawolle, 2004). We will now move on to an examination of the PISA effect on the national context, by looking at the examples of Finland, Germany and the United Kingdom. Finland, having done exceptionally well in the full PISA cycle, is still basking in the glory of these positive results. Germany, in contrast, was encouraged to undertake urgent educational reforms. Finally, the UK case reveals some interesting differences between Scotland and England in relation to PISA.

The Case of Finland

The outstanding success of Finnish students in PISA has been a great joy but at the same time a somewhat puzzling experience to all those responsible for and making decisions about education in Finland. At a single stroke, PISA has transformed our conceptions of the quality of the work done at our comprehensive school and of the foundations it has laid for Finland's future civilization and development of knowledge. Traditionally, we have been used to thinking that the models for educational reforms have to be taken from abroad. For a long time, we thus turned to Germany for these models ... Today, thanks to PISA, the situation seems suddenly to have changed, with Finnish schooling and Finnish school practices in the focus of the international attention.
(Välijärvi et al, 2002, p. 3)

Indeed, 'the Finnish miracle of PISA' (Simola, 2005) has been at the centre of international attention since the first PISA results were published in 2001. Even though the PISA success was initially received within the country with great surprise ('from a country following the examples of others to one serving as a model for others' [Välijärvi et al, 2002, p. 3]), the Finnish Ministry of Education was soon to attribute the positive results to an education system that offers both high quality and equality to its students (Finnish Ministry of Education, 2007).

According to Välijärvi et al, non-differentiation is the secret of the success of the Finnish comprehensive school. Instead of tracking and streaming, Finnish teachers are in a position to cater for the needs of individual students. This is thanks to the 'highly educated, a pedagogical expert' (2002, p. 42) Finnish teacher, who is generally regarded very highly in Finnish society. In addition, due to the absence of any national tests or examinations upon completion of compulsory schooling, teachers' assessment of their pupils is all the more important. Finland does have national grading guidelines for performance but, according to the Finnish PISA team, these are flexible and allow for a broad definition of student achievement (Välijärvi et al, 2002). Teachers in Finland take decisions themselves in regard to the textbooks they are going to use; the early 1990s reform of the curriculum brought greater curricular flexibility and pedagogical freedom than ever before. Therefore, the official reporting of the country's PISA results supports the conclusion that comprehensive schooling, in addition to teacher autonomy and motivation, were the decisive factors in the high performance of Finnish students. In terms of the ways that PISA results were received by the Finnish government and media, it is remarkable that the Finnish press was found to have mentioned the country's success in only eight pages, whereas Germany, one of the lowest performers, received 687 pages of press attention (European Network, 2004). Interestingly, the announcement of the results of an international assessment of this magnitude was received with neutrality by the media and perhaps with surprise by the Finnish government, which apparently decided to move into announcing further reforms, despite the almost global acclaim for the existing system. PISA seems to have been used here to mobilize policy action aimed at securing constant improvement against the country's results:

> Paradoxically, shortly after the international publication of the first PISA results, the Finnish government made a decision to harmonise the education system by adding to the share of compulsory studies in comprehensive schools and by giving more weight to core subjects ... Assessment results and political decision making on education do not always go hand in hand. (Välijärvi et al, 2002, p.44)

The Case of Germany

The results of PISA 2000 had a major effect on Germany's education system. Rankings that placed it 20th in reading, mathematical and scientific literacy among 32 countries were a severe shock to policy makers, school teachers and parents. The negative results dominated the German media, which presented them in almost all newspapers. Project leaders gave several interviews, experts offered their interpretations and roundtable television discussions were also held (European Network, 2004). In response to the PISA findings, German education authorities organized a conference of ministers in 2002 and proposed reforms of an urgent nature, such as developing standards for measuring students' competencies upon completion of secondary schooling and the introduction of large-scale assessment testing at the end of primary and secondary education.

Teachers were under increasing pressure, especially with the delivery of new reform measures, and urgent measures were deemed necessary to focus the system more on outputs rather than inputs and to develop standards regarding skills upon completion of school and entry into the labour market. Despite criticisms of the PISA testing frame and statistical validity that came from within the country (see Wuttke, 2006), new projects were initiated. Some of them, in direct response to the PISA testing model, were Chemie im Kontext (CHIK), Physik im Kontext (PIKO) and SINUS (Steigerung der Effizienz des mathematisches-naturwissenschaftlichen Unterrichts) (Federal Ministry of Education and Research). Further, the PISA-Konsortium Deutschland produced reports on the development of the competencies of German pupils (Prenzel et al, 2004). Finally, national tests of learning outcomes in core subjects were also introduced for the first time. What we see here appears to be a common phenomenon in relation to PISA results and their reportage: an initial critique of the statistics themselves and a questioning of their validity, but then an apparent acceptance of the data and appropriate policy responses to the situation as defined by these data. Pongratz (2006) maintains that no other empirical study managed to stir up the educational policy landscape in Germany in the way that PISA 2000 did. He compares the 'flood' of discussions and reform measures that PISA brought with the crisis scenarios that German education experienced in the 1960s, and particularly what was then called the *Bildungskatastrophe* (Pongratz, 2006). According to him, the 'PISA-shock' has had a major impact not only on policy making, but most crucially on the public consciousness. However, he states:

> This result is clearly cause for critical self-reflection, but it is
> not in itself a sufficient basis for the frantic radicalism of the
> resultant reform measures. It seems that something is
> operating through reform strategies of diverse types that has

the capacity to exercise enormous pressure. This pressure functions as a strategic element within a currently active global transformation process driven by a wide variety of organisations and actors. (Pongratz, 2006, p. 472)

The PISA results, apart from curricular reforms, brought a whole new conceptualization of the German school as a self-managing organization, in need of new quality control measures, applied in different combinations by the federal states: school inspections, self-evaluations, assessment tests and teacher professionalization have turned the German education system into a peculiar mixture of centralization and decentralization.

The Case of the United Kingdom

PISA is administered separately in England, Scotland and Northern Ireland (Wales is included in the English sample), but the United Kingdom is regarded as a single national entity by the OECD for the PISA purposes. The then Department for Education and Skills (DfES – since renamed the Department for Children, Schools and Families [DSCF], and from 2010 the Department for Education) commissioned the Social Survey Division of the Office for National Statistics (ONS) to carry out the study in England. The Social Survey Division also conducted the survey in Northern Ireland, in collaboration with the Central Survey Unit of the Northern Ireland Statistics and Research Agency. The Northern Ireland survey was commissioned by the Department of Education Northern Ireland (DENI). Finally, the Scottish Executive commissioned the Scottish Council for Research in Education (SCRE, University of Glasgow) to conduct the study in Scotland. In both PISA 2000 and 2003, England had difficulty in reaching the required response rates, in order to be included in the survey, arguably due to the large amount of data collection already demanded of schools. However, media in the UK showed very high interest, reporting the results with headlines such as 'School is far more fun in Scotland', 'Teenagers are world-beaters when it comes to maths and science', etc. (European Network, 2004). In contrast to the press in other countries, the UK media did not report the negative elements of the results extensively. In particular, the significant gap between the performance of pupils from well-off and deprived backgrounds that was to be found in both the 2000 and 2003 surveys did not attract media attention at all. On the day of the publication of the 2000 results, PISA generated nine prominent national newspaper lead stories and featured in the national news twice on that day and several times by the end of the week. Tony Blair, the then UK Prime Minister, commented on the PISA 2000 results on the day of the publication in the House of Commons: 'The country should be very proud of the OECD survey, which is a tribute to the hard work of pupils, heads, teachers, governors and parents across the country' (European Network, 2004, p. 13). In PISA 2000, the United Kingdom took 7th position in reading literacy, 8th position in mathematical literacy and 4th position in scientific literacy. The DfES produced booklets summarizing the findings for teachers and head teachers and distributed them electronically through 'Teachernet', the Department's website for teachers and heads of schools. Finally, teachers' unions held a conference on the PISA 2000 findings in 2003, which was very well attended by teachers, policy makers from the DfES, OECD representatives and politicians (including David Miliband, then Secretary of State) (Teachernet, 2007). A DfES/DCSF official, commenting on media interest in PISA, noted its significance as a 'brand':

> I think PISA probably gets the most attention and that's not because it is any more valid or reliable, it is simply because OECD has done such a brilliant marketing job with PISA. So it is a real brand name, ministers are familiar with it, politicians generally are familiar with it, the press, the education press and beyond are all familiar with PISA. (Interview with English policy actor, December 2008)

No concrete initiatives were undertaken in the UK – in either England or Scotland – in response to PISA results. The same DfES/DCSF official saw no impact on policy at national level, but wondered if practices in England were influencing international systems because of England's success:

> At the national level? I don't think we've noticed that, we are not changing our systems in any particular way to accommodate ... maybe the other way round is happening. I don't know. No, I don't think we got such thing going on ... . At the policy level it was more of an affirmation that we were on the right track, except that we could do better in terms of equity. At the political level a great deal was made of it because you know it was looking pretty good stuff. (Interview with English policy actor, December 2008)

In Scotland, the Scottish Executive published a report for PISA 2000 through its Education and Young People Research Unit (Scottish Executive Education Department, 2002). According to it, in PISA 2000:

> Scotland was in the top third of countries in all subjects assessed. The results indicated that Scotland's 15 year olds performed significantly better in terms of attainment in mathematics and science than our 9 and 13 year olds did in earlier international studies, and this is likely to be the case in reading too. (Scottish Executive Education Department, 2002, p. 3)

In the Scottish Executive report, the analysis of the results ranges from examining PISA results in general, to looking at the performance of the United Kingdom and sometimes offering Scotland-specific comments. These are mainly used to justify and reinforce the reasoning for measures and policies already under way. For instance, according to the report, the relationship between students' views on the school climate and students' performance was considered significant and thus supportive of 'the emphasis in Scotland in recent years through school self evaluation and the Ethos Network' (Scottish Executive, 2002, p. 12). Interviews with members of the Inspectorate and the Executive's Analytical Services Division point to a strategic use of PISA to establish Scotland in the wider world:

> But I think it's partly about you know this is putting Scotland on the map. We do quite well in PISA so what more can we extract from that by way of evidence on our position in the world. (Interview with Scottish policy actor, June 2008)

In addition, PISA is a source of reassurance to policy makers in Scotland, especially in relation to their adherence to a different model of quality assurance and evaluation from that in England, with no national testing, and an inspection regime that promotes self-evaluation:

> we have the reassurance of PISA for example, suggesting that overall our students are, on average reasonably pretty high performing anyway. The PISA data I don't think could be seen as a huge driver in the inspection model, because it is favourable for Scotland. There wouldn't be any particular basis for saying, oh because of PISA we must do this or that. (Interview with Scottish policy actor, July 2008)

Having briefly examined three national 'cases' as examples of the ways PISA enters the domestic front and impacts on national education systems in Europe, it is interesting to move on to examine the views of European policy makers operating at the level of Brussels. What are their views about the impact of PISA on European education systems? How has PISA contributed to the dominance of evidence-based policy making in the European Commission? Building on findings from in-depth interviews with two key policy actors from the European Commission and its agencies, namely the Research, Indicators and Analysis Division in the Directorate-General for Education and Culture and Eurydice, the next section examines the impact of PISA on policy making at the European level and especially in relation to the shaping and steering of education policy transnationally.

PISA and Europe

We support OECD in carrying out a number of surveys by supporting member states. We pay 80% of the national costs by the budget of the Union ... We have meetings very regularly and we have even joined projects now. We work very closely with them on evidence-based policy making. (Interview with Commission official, September 2007)

50-60% of the data for the EU's indicators report for the Lisbon strategy are from the OECD, yes. And of course are the same. (Interview with ex-Eurydice staff member, March 2007)

International organizations such as the OECD and the European Union should not be seen as monolithic institutions but as part of the 'global architecture of education', described by Jones (2007) as 'a complex web of ideas, networks of influence, policy frameworks and practices, financial arrangements and organizational structures' (p. 326). According to the Eurydice actor quoted above, the European Commission is highly dependent on PISA data, first, because it pays substantially for it, and secondly because collaboration on data collection between the two international organizations has increased significantly over recent years:

And we also work with OECD because the OECD is the main coordinator for the UOE [UNESCO/OECD/European Union] data which is 60% of the data that we use in such a report and that means that we participate in all the meetings of INES [Indicators of Education Systems], the scientific committees of OECD. We go to all these meetings and we have a seat and agreement with the OECD, a formal, very formal, an official agreement that the Commission has a seat in all their committees. (Interview with Commission official, September 2007)

So those involved in the collection of data at European level or at the international level in OECD tend to be more and more closely related. Also because at EU level it would cost too much money to develop such instruments like PISA. So of course you have to cooperate and I think it is good because there is no extra money to spend – it is the philosophy that is different that we argued and I think this is still the case. The corpus of data is the same, OECD, Eurostat and UNESCO, they share the data but then when you look at the products and what you do with the data, makes the difference. And where you use it. (Interview with ex-Eurydice staff member, March 2007)

PISA has been a major instrument in providing data on the European education systems and in shaping the ways that European experts and networks operate and the policy areas they focus on. For example, in relation to the European Commission's relatively newly-established 'peer learning activities' [10], PISA seems to be shaping interests and travel itineraries across Europe:

> The agenda is to better understand what Finland is doing to succeed in PISA. What do they do? Specialised teaching or individualised teaching? So they go to Finland, these experts, not just to travel, they go to Finland in order to best understand what Finland is doing. Can the Finnish experience actually inspire something to be done in England –which will be an English decision and an English matter. So this transfer of experiences is very complex and very difficult because what is in the mind of people is if I transfer a system, will that work? To identify the elements of success that are relevant to your country and which can be used in your country and have roots in your system, that's very very difficult and we don't have the methodology for doing it. But we can at least go from this logic of identifying objectively one way or another good performance and then approach an understanding of why and how they do that. Then inspire other countries to at least reflect what they can learn from that. (Interview with Commission official, September 2007)

What is not challenged here is the explicit policy orientation PISA has, on the basis of which its data are being collected. PISA data in Europe seem to be a given – the problem appears to be how to deal with them. PISA is seen as an objective assessment of 'good' or 'bad' performance that currently lacks contextualization and that more 'traditional' European policy instruments, such as European networks and policy experts, can work on. Interestingly, these policy transfer mechanisms appear to be losing ground ('My critique is that I don't believe intellectually they have the methodology for looking at anything. They look at things that shine' [Interview with Commission official, September 2007]). OECD technical expertise, and PISA in particular, has become the impetus for a drive in the European Commission towards establishing its own technical capacity – this is not just a question of producing better or more relevant data. It is a political decision, which relates to education markets and the development of statistical expertise at sites much closer to home:

> We see the very big reports they publish and it is always Australians, Canadians, Americans that run away with the money. Always. It is ACER [Australian Council for Educational Research] that is the Australian one, ACER that

sits on the big contracts of analysis on PISA or TIMSS or whatever national survey, they sit on it. This has been a problem for Europe, for European countries for many years. Especially France that protests, they say this is Anglo-Saxon, American controlled organisation, we don't want it. Therefore we should develop a European capability of doing these things. It was in view to do this with the language indicator which is a very big contract, 6 million, that we are doing this year. We reflected on how can we develop a capability of European research institutes to compete in this field, so we are not giving money to Australians, Canadians, how do we develop the competence of doing such big competences at the European level? (Interview with ex-Eurydice staff member, March 2007)

Analysing the narratives of the two European policy makers quoted in this chapter, one can clearly feel a tension; with the dominance (and quality) of PISA data taken for granted, the discussion focuses on its impact. There is an evident split between focusing on PISA data and its policy directions in order to look at specific issues where standards need to be raised and equity gaps closed, and the opinion of those who find PISA data useful, but feel that the 'philosophy' and principles of governing European education cannot be reduced to the results of one testing instrument. For example:

This report gives the information but it doesn't focus [*shows a Eurydice report*], it doesn't give policy directions. So if you cut down, personally I would go down to one indicator. That would change according to the agenda, but now it is school drop-outs. For me, drop-outs or low performance in literacy in PISA. (Interview with Commission official, March 2007)

However, from a different viewpoint:

The ranking of countries is not a problem at the OECD level. It is in the EU. So I would say the corpus of data is the same [but] ... OECD has its own product, the EU has its own product because it has a different philosophy and a different approach. Not harmonisation of the systems but diversity, working as I said with the convergences using the research results. (Interview with ex-Eurydice staff member, March 2007)

Finally, it seems important for the European Commission to maintain a balanced approach to the emphasis and weight they give to surveys from other international organizations, such as the IEA, as well:

We participate around all discussions around PISA and around TIMSS and we are very critical of seeing PISA as the ultimate answer of what counts in education. It is a tool amongst others, it measures with some instruments that can be improved, our people manage to use it to do something. We think that we need to have a much better understanding of what we look at when we look at PISA data and we have argued that we should do that by looking at what TIMSS does. Not replace the one with the other but look at them together. (Interview with Commission official, September 2007)

Discussion

The logic of the growing policy space in education had moved away from the considered and careful, perhaps sometimes slow and ineffectual, growth of pre-millennium education policy across Europe. It was driven by the need to manage European growth and accession, new areas and new objectives, and global challenges. Individual countries, managing their own progress, used any resource they could or that they felt they should, and the OECD and its PISA programme became of greater importance.

At the same time, the importance of benchmarks, indicators and rankings became the dominant way of governing, and led to exponential growth of data collection, its devices and its exclusions.

Instruments at work are not neutral devices: they produce specific effects, independently of the objective pursued ... which structure public policy according to their own logic. (Lascoumes & Le Galès, 2007, p. 3)

This chapter has attempted to illustrate quite different PISA 'results', both at the national and the transnational level: from the PISA-surprise of Finland, to the PISA-shock of Germany, the PISA-promotion of the United Kingdom and the focus by the European Commission on the possibilities PISA data have created. What is constant is the acceptance of PISA – and the parameters and direction that it establishes – along with its incorporation into domestic and European policy making.

In particular, PISA data are used to justify change or provide support for existing policy direction in both the domestic and the European contexts (even in England with its long-term investment in high-stakes testing and its highly sophisticated system of data production and use). Europe has found in PISA a valuable source of data about the systems it is meant to govern. However, political choices, such as who produces these data and their cost, how one uses these data to understand different education histories and political contexts, and finally, how one strikes a balance between the levels of cooperation with other international organizations such as the IEA, seem to be issues of great concern.

Responsiveness to PISA across the different participating nations and by other international organizations can be seen as an instance of what Luhmann has called 'externalisation' (Luhmann & Schorr, 1979, quoted in Steiner-Khamsi, 2004). That is, the reference to 'world situations' enables policy makers to make the case for education reforms at home that would otherwise be contested. Thus, 'local' policy actors are using PISA as a form of domestic policy legitimation, or as a means of defusing discussion by presenting policy as based on robust evidence. The local policy actor also signals, to an international audience, through PISA, the adherence of their nation to reform agendas (Steiner-Khamsi, 2004, p. 76), and thus joins the club of competitive nations. Moreover, the construction of PISA with its promotion of orientations to applied and lifelong learning has powerful effects on curricula and pedagogy in participating nations, and promotes the responsible individual and self-regulated subject.

Finally, PISA is a major governing resource for Europe: it provides knowledge and information about systems, and implants constant comparison within the EU member states – without the need for new or explicit forms of regulation in education. With Europeanization being understood as having the potential to be simultaneously a response to, as well as a conduit of, globalization (Rosamond, 2003), PISA clearly seems to constitute an important node in the complex task of governing European education. This reading of PISA supports this chapter's overarching argument about its use and meaning as a political technology: a governing resource for both the national agency and the transnational forces of the EU and the OECD.

CHAPTER 9

School Self-evaluation as Travelling Policy across Europe: the role of the Scottish Inspectorate and SICI

Introduction

The European space for education, as we have tried to show, has many actors and sites of work, often working to produce a regional imaginary and a professional solidarity. Policies travel across this space and shape it. Associations and their networks can be vital in this process. This chapter is focused on the way that practices spread, and why they travel (when others may not).

One of these policy ideas in education, growing out of Scottish practice, is school self-evaluation, which has travelled from Scotland and the Scottish inspectors of education to a number of European countries through SICI, the Standing International Conference of Inspectorates. The translation of self-evaluation across Europe reveals the tension between data and judgement in systems which are using regulatory data more and more, and the way in which 'hard' data and expert judgement are now increasingly being dissolved, with hard data opening up to 'soft' measures (like the measurement of creativity and innovation), while expert judgement becomes more standardized as it needs to be brought in line with similar judgements in other contexts – in other words, it needs to be comparable in order to flow.

School Self-evaluation (SSE) is the focus of this chapter because it represents the culmination of a long process of Europe-wide policy developments aimed at the improvement of school performance; however, at the same time, it offers a 'break' from these developments, as it shifts the focus from the regulation of performance associated with external mechanisms such as inspection and examination success rates, to a focus on the whole school and its redesign as a learning organization. This increasingly influential school of thought sees members of learning organizations as contributing added value through their continuous learning, which generates new, productive, knowledge, not for the individual learner, but for the organization (OECD, 2000). This approach, it is argued, also reduces costs, because it is less reliant on external mechanisms to monitor performance, while engendering relations of trust, transparency and openness within the organization, that are conducive to 'real' learning. The regulatory regimes associated with 'new public management' had, of course, been criticized in terms of their costs and their installation of performative cultures of distrust within organizations, so the promotion of SSE by European inspectorates may be understood as a response to those problems, and also as a logical development from them, in that the installation of performance measures made it possible – once benchmarks had been installed – to move towards an emphasis on self-regulation.

European inspectorates are also faced with other new challenges that, in some ways, not only question their traditional authority in delivering school assessment but sometimes threaten them by rendering them obsolete; on the one hand, they are faced with increasing school autonomy in relation to schools' own evaluation of learning and teaching, with schools (at least in some contexts) sometimes questioning the extent to which the inspection process offers anything more than a disruption to the life of the school. On the other, due to the proliferation of data and the increasing broadening of learning lifelong and life-wide, their traditional, almost 'old-worldly' status as classroom connoisseurs is also questioned; rather than derive clout from their historical position, today they increasingly need to appear fresh, cutting edge, and outward-looking. Therefore, this chapter works with the idea about how previously powerful, largely disconnected policy communities now need to come together to redefine and modernize what they do – and above all, protect their internal, local standing – by seeking support and ideas externally. We do not claim that these developments apply to the same degree to all inspectorates in Europe; however, we do argue that to *some* degree most inspectorates in Europe are moving in this same direction. Thus, the focus of this chapter is on the significance of European associations like SICI in the travelling of these ideas and their embedding in new contexts. The next section focuses on the Scottish Inspectorate and gives a brief history of the development of self-evaluation in Scotland before it travelled abroad.

From the View of the Local: school self-evaluation in Scotland

In 1991, the Audit Unit of the Scottish Inspectorate began advocating the use of development planning, with the publication of *The Role of School Development Plans in Managing School Effectiveness* (Scottish Office Education Department [SOED], 1991a). This document was accompanied by the distribution to secondary schools of what was described as a staff development package, *Using Examination Results in School Self evaluation: relative ratings and national comparison factors* (SOED, 1991b), together with 'Standard Tables' – a package of statistical information about examination performance per school. The Standard Tables were subsequently issued each year and compared performance by subject departments within a school (Relative Ratings), and school departmental performance with national figures (National Comparison Factors) (Cowie et al, 2007). This was the first attempt at developing the self-evaluation regime in Scotland, the new policy paradigm of measuring, describing and assessing education. Comparison and competition through data would from now on become major features for the inspection of schools.

The methodology of development planning was pushed further through Circular No. 1/94 (SOED, 1994a, p. 1), which provided further guidelines for schools and education authorities 'in line with the objective of the Parents' Charter to improve quality and standards in Scottish Schools'. Education authorities were expected to make arrangements to support development planning in schools and ensure that each school produced an annual plan in accordance with advice contained in the guidelines. Updated advice on development planning focused on quality assurance, which was said to be dependent on 'systematic professional evaluation of the achievement of clearly defined aims by the school's own staff led by the head teacher' (SOED, 1994b, p. 1). Development planning was described as an enabling mechanism through which change and improvement could be planned, introduced and consolidated, and a linkage was made between development planning and effectiveness by demonstrating how performance indicators may be used in self-evaluation.

The processes of self-evaluation and development planning were set out more explicitly by the Audit Unit publication, *How Good is Our School? Self-evaluation Using Performance Indicators* (HGIOS) (Scottish Office Education and Industry Department [SOEID], 1996). HGIOS provided a set of performance indicators of what a good school should look like – overtly based on perceived characteristics of effective schools. HGIOS replaced the earlier material on the use of indicators, and provided a comprehensive list of performance indicators, which were said to be based on good practice at school, local authority and national levels. According to the foreword to the first publication of HGIOS, there was now concerted effort to move closer to the 'local', answering the local question, 'How good is our school?'. HGIOS suggests that although indicators had given a 'head start' to Scotland 'in its drive to improve standards and quality in education', this 'refined set' of indicators would now 'keep Scotland at the forefront of developments worldwide' (SOEID, 1996, p. v). According to the Scottish Office, HGIOS would help:

teachers and head teachers to improve pupils' performance
and to answer the questions put to them by parents,
employers, directors of education and HM Inspectors' about:
– How well are pupils performing?
– How effective is the school?
– How well is the school managed and led?
– What are the school's key strengths?
– What are the main points for action?
(SOEID, 1996)

This was one of the first attempts to collapse the division between school evaluation carried out by teachers and external assessment done by the Inspectorate. Indicators offered both parties a common language in order to discuss 'how are we doing?', 'how do we know?' and 'what are we going to do now?' Thus, HGIOS became the tool to promote a progressive form of self-evaluation, developed, however, in the 'bullet-point' logic of prescribed steps that teachers and head teachers had to go through, and measured through specific performance indicators already used by Her Majesty's Inspectorate of Education (HMIE). A number of further publications provided supporting materials and case studies of self-evaluation, as the Inspectorate urged and cajoled schools to use their methodology.

However, in the political climate of the 1990s the reactions of schools and local authorities to all aspects of quality assurance were coloured by distrust of policies considered to be ideological impositions by the UK Conservative government, which had no political support in Scotland. Thus, in many schools self-evaluation tended to be regarded as a charade (Cowie, 2001). Following the change in UK political control from Conservative to New Labour in 1997, there was more rhetoric about 'partnership' in policy documents, but also more pressure on schools to implement quality assurance procedures and meet performance targets.

In 1997, HMIE set out its vision for working in partnership with local authorities and schools through the Quality Initiative in Scottish Schools (SOEID, 1997). Each participating authority was expected to set a policy framework for quality assurance, engage in the analysis of the available evidence of school performance and work towards producing a report on standards and quality reflecting the context of the authority. At school level, schools were expected to have development plans in place, show commitment to improvement through self-evaluation, and work towards producing some form of school standards and quality report. The education authority was expected to support, moderate and validate these processes. Target setting across the key areas identified in HGIOS was seen as an important element in the initiative. Responses of schools and local authorities to the initiative varied, and in 1999 an HMIE report on the management of quality improvement in education authorities suggested that implementation of the quality assurance and evaluation methodology was quite patchy (SOEID, 1999).

As indicated above, the Standards in Scotland's Schools etc. Act set out statutory requirements for school improvement within an improvement framework encompassing a set of five National Priorities (Scottish Parliament, 2000). A series of performance indicators was identified for each priority and education authorities were expected to agree targets for achievement of these indicators with their schools, very much in line with UK policy direction and development.

However, HGIOS positions the Inspectorate as guide and enabler of 'home-grown' quality assurance processes that are built and maintained by the school, using HMIE guidance. In the Inspectorate's view, schools may welcome periodic inspections that 'they are keeping up to the HMIE mark' (Weir, 2008, p. 148). HMIE thus may be able to recover its position, and through HGIOS and other policies relating to self-evaluation, become a key actor in the production of new kinds of knowledge about Scottish education. By offering the tools for encoding knowledge about classroom practice, HMIE influenced and continues to influence the production of knowledge for policy, as well as its production in more general terms by schools as educational establishments. The Inspectorate has played the double role of the shaper of policy as well as the mediator between central government and the classroom. The Inspectorate is a Janus-like profession; inspectors always face both ways – to the government and to the school. Depending on the political context and circumstances, its mediating powers are at times diminished and at other times increased.

To conclude, self-evaluation has provided the Scottish Inspectorate with a possible means of recovering its status and role, and offered a paradigm shift that it can claim to have generated and which enables it to identify with a 'learning' government in a 'learning' system. Indeed self-evaluation has enabled the Inspectorate to expand into other areas of provision, one of which is that of 'teaching' SSE to other inspectorates in Europe. Returning to the core focus of this chapter, SSE also provided the Inspectorate with an agenda for policy teaching, taking it to other European countries, and bringing it back strengthened, and thus consolidating the Inspectorate's position. Inspectors have a reinvigorated function, as those with the expertise and capacity to create those frameworks and a common language for schools to evaluate themselves. They are also the intelligence gatherers, using self-evaluation techniques as a means of translating and interpreting the system to government, and to the new 'partners' in government.

SSE as a Travelling Policy: the role of SICI

An interesting element of the SSE approach is the way in which it is presented as essentially 'Scottish': as somehow encapsulating elements of Scottish practices and approaches that reflect particular choices and priorities. In this sense SICI is referencing a hinterland of supposedly shared purposes that may derive ultimately from principles of the Scottish Enlightenment and from Calvinistic Protestantism. By this we mean that SICI actors assume that improvement through self-knowledge and effort is both possible and desirable – indeed self-improvement is a duty.

This branding of SSE as the 'Scottish approach' has undoubtedly helped in its rapid take-up within and beyond Scotland, as it has been successfully exported to many other European countries (including England), which are looking to Scotland for examples of how to train more 'self-aware' and thus self-managed teachers. Therefore we also examine self-evaluation as a Scottish but also an increasingly European policy shift. We make a case for how travelling policies, when becoming international, return home reinvigorated, and more widely accepted and unquestioned than ever before. In other words, the scrutiny of scrutiny at the level of the international is what makes a policy shift solid and impervious to resistance or doubt. Hence, apart from achieving international prestige and recognition (and policy elites like the Inspectorate are always in need of these kinds of power displays), previous knowledge and policy constellations become far easier to mould and recast into new relationships and valued/devalued knowledge forms. Through the systematic efforts of the key knowledge actors, the Scottish Inspectorate, revised and improved versions of the self-evaluation policy paradigm point towards further refinement of the tools and show the intricate ways in which new knowledge categories (and processes of knowledge production) begin to matter, especially at times of financial crisis in the public sector and shrinking budgets. This chapter will focus on an exploration of the processes, as well as the actors, organizations and scenes of policy making that relate this.

SICI: the beginnings

The Standing International Conference of Inspectorates (SICI) serves as a forum for exchanging experience in relation to inspection systems and wider education issues across Europe. In the articles of its foundation in 1995, SICI stated the following aims: sharing experience; updating developments regarding education systems; finding ways to improve working methods; and establishing a basis for cooperation between the various school authorities. Nevertheless, what is not discussed in that foundational document are the more interesting questions: why was there a need to establish a forum where European inspectorates meet? What were the reasons for previously well-established, powerful policy communities to start looking 'out'?

An answer to these questions might come from two directions: first, the role of specific actors in pushing local and national agendas at the international stage; and second, a general feeling that inspectorates needed to modernize to retain their former status. In 1997, Douglas Osler, Chief Inspector and leader of the Scottish Inspectorate, was elected President of SICI; during his time, SICI grew through the organization of workshops, the development of a series of studies on the inspection of schools in Europe, the compiling of critical analyses of school inspection in Europe and the instigation of mutual projects which were based on joint visits or joint inspections. What we observe as a first attempt to organize the work of SICI are features that would continue and be strengthened in the years to come: SICI was not simply an association that was run through meetings – rather, it was active in promoting specific agendas through the organization of workshops, where both teaching of 'best' practices and learning were taking place, as well as conducting specific studies, in order to acquire 'evidence'. Osler, in his speech at the International SICI Congress in Utrecht in 2000, spoke about 'The future of school inspectorates in the 21st century', stressing for the first time that inspecting was not enough any more – there was now a need to focus on continuous improvement, and that improvement could only come from working together (SICI Newsletter, 2000).

From its foundation in 1995 SICI became involved in a number of interesting studies and exchanges of expertise in inspectorates; however, it is since 2000 that the association appears to have become more active and has even attempted to instigate collaborations with international organizations, who are invited to meetings, such as the OECD and the European Commission. Interestingly, in a SICI meeting for the celebration of the 200th anniversary of the Netherlands Inspectorate in 2001, Tersmette, a representative of the Education policy unit of the Directorate-General Education and Culture, suggested that a new era had just began with the arrival of the open method of coordination and the launch of indicators and benchmarking for education policy in Europe. He called it 'a silent revolution' and argued that it would be a 'new frontier for European integration', comparing it with the completion of the internal market, the introduction of the Euro and the enlargement of the Union (Tersmette, 2001). Tersmette emphasized the new significance given to education by the Lisbon Strategy – 'so what the Lisbon agenda does, is that it places typical education and training issues firmly back in the hands of education and training authorities themselves' (2001, n.p.) – and that the work of associations such as SICI was crucial in this process as, he suggested, there was a need 'not only to close performance gaps between countries, but rather to close communication gaps'. Further, he contended that

> I believe that when we start debating and comparing quality
> issues in education, the process counts perhaps more than the

> results. It is about agreeing on terminology, on concepts, finding common ground, speaking common language. (2001, n.p.)

This was an area formerly underdeveloped in European inspectorates and a gap that SICI had to fill. The realization of the need to 'find common ground', as Tersmette suggested, did not only come to SICI and its founders; more and more inspectorates from across Europe would now register as members with the association. By 2002 SICI was already an organization of 20 member countries, and also had associate members who were allowed to participate in SICI for two years without paying the required fee (in 2011, 3000 Euros). Some of its main functions remained the organization of workshops, which 'have formed the backbone' (SICI, 2003, p. 6) of SICI, as they 'provide opportunities to discuss and analyse key aspects of education and inspection ... also [they] provide opportunities to develop the valuable personal contacts that can be built into partnerships' (SICI, 2003, p. 6).

One of the main developments during the first years after the establishment of SICI was the production of what was called the Blue Book or the 'Inspectorates of Education in Europe' book, compiled by the Flemish DVO (Dienest Voor Onderwijsontwikkeling/ Department for Educational Development) with the aim to provide a quick overview of European inspectorates. An act of inscription, the information given in the 'Book' was for the first time collected and put together with the aim to map out but also compile a record of identity and purpose – a collective inscription. The effort began in 1998 and the descriptive mapping covered 14 countries, the then members of SICI. Some of the themes developed in the book are the organization of the inspectorate; its areas of responsibility; the process of inspection, as well as its methods (frameworks, indicators and criteria for data gathering); the relation between inspectorate evaluation and self-evaluation of schools; and instruments and methods – the way inspectors collect information and the approaches they use when carrying out their work. Although printed to start with, the Blue Book was soon developed into a web database which could be searched (and still is) both by country and also thematically.

Further, newsletters are produced up to four times a year by the Secretariat, covering a wide range of inspection-related topics. All members – and other inspectors, on occasion – are invited to contribute short papers or articles for these newsletters, as well as to inform members about the work of the Executive Committee and the General Assembly.

Self-Evaluation and SICI

The 'Effective School Self-Evaluation' project (ESSE) has been one of the most significant projects SICI has undertaken. Funded by the European Commission, the ESSE project ran for two years (2001-3) and had the following aims:

- Identify key indicators for evaluating the effectiveness of school self-evaluation;
- Develop a methodology for inspecting school self-evaluation;
- Identify the weaknesses of school self-evaluation across countries and regions;
- Produce an analysis of how self-evaluation and external evaluation can most effectively be combined; and
- Produce case studies of effective self-evaluation in practice.

Thirteen European countries and regions took part in the project, which comprised mainly of a questionnaire survey, as well as documentation and personal contacts. The combined use of these sources led to the development of a draft case study for each participating region which was later sent to the respondents in order to check for accuracy of the information supplied. The questionnaire dealt with a series of issues such as the statutory position of self-evaluation in the different countries/regions; benchmarking; indicators, standards, criteria and conceptual frameworks to evaluate the quality of school self-evaluation; stakeholders in the school self-evaluation process; the role of the inspectorate; external inspection of the quality and effectiveness of the schools' self-evaluation process; and other similar areas (European Commission-SICI, 2001).

Chris Webb, from HMIE in Scotland, was the manager of the project. During the SICI ESSE workshop in Copenhagen in 2005, which, according to Erik Nexelmann, the Head of Division in the Danish Ministry of Education, was a 'milestone in the ESSE project' (SICI, 2005), Webb stated that the project took as its starting point the European Union's strategic target for 2010 to be the most competitive, dynamic and knowledge-based economy in the world. According to Webb, this target required a modernization of the education systems in Europe; it called for inspections across Europe to play a role in encouraging transparency, quality evaluation and self-evaluation. Webb also stressed that 'school self-evaluation does not exist in a vacuum, but in a context where external support and benchmarks are important' (SICI, 2005). The external support, for Webb, can be found in the form of statistical data for comparison, sets of quality standards and training in self-evaluation methods. Webb listed the features of schools with 'high capacity' as those which promote leadership, reflective and systematic self-evaluation and systematic tracking and evaluation of pupils' progress. Finally, the ESSE project manager stressed the need for balance between self-evaluation and external evaluation, 'to prevent schools ... resulting to self-delusion' (SICI, 2005).

The final report from the project outlines the 'ESSE framework' (SICI, 2003) which provides the rationale behind self-evaluation and sets out the quality indicators (QIs), which range from level 4 (very good) to level 1 (unsatisfactory). These indicators are applied in what are described as the following 'key areas':

Key Area 1 – Vision and strategy
QI 1.1 Aims and values
QI 1.2 Strategy and policy for self-evaluation and improvement

Key Area 2 – Evaluation and improvement of key inputs
QI 2.1 Staff/human resources

Key Area 3 – Evaluation and improvement of key processes
QI 3.1 Policies, guidelines and standards
QI 3.2 Planning and implementation of self-evaluation activities
QI 3.3 Planning and implementation of action for improvement

Key Area 4 – Evaluation and impact on outcomes
QI 4.1 Evaluation and improvement of key outcomes
QI 4.2 Impact of self-evaluation on improving key outcomes

The report provides guidelines for conducting evaluation visits using the above framework of quality indicators, explores the balance between internal and external evaluation and contains country reports which set out the strengths in self-evaluation in the countries/regions that participated in the project. Finally, the report features case studies of effective school self-evaluation.

The Scottish contribution to the ESSE project has been crucial. This is not only to be seen in the similarities of the recommendations of the final project report to quality indicators set in the 'How Good is Our School' reports, but crucially through the personal contacts and travelling of ideas and people from Scotland to the other participating countries. According to a Scottish policy actor describing in general the position of Scotland within the European education space and specifically in relation to the concept of self-evaluation:

> Well, we feed back to people. We find a lot of the time we are ... this sounds slightly odd, but we're actually giving more than we're necessarily taking out. Partly because of the sort of area of work in which we are ... particularly with the accession nations that we're actually, in a sense, ahead of the game in Scotland ... we have, for instance, presented on what we do in Scotland. And that's caused considerable interest and they've come back to us and asked for more. ... Well on the entire self-evaluation system in Scotland. ... So how, you know, how

inspection fits with evaluation. Some of these countries have inspectorates, some don't. So they're always interested in that relationship. They're interested in what the expectations of schools are. (Interview with Scottish policy maker, June 2008)

Interviewees were keen to express the unique contribution of Scotland to other European nations, often in juxtaposition to their English counterparts. Indeed, one could evidence an almost anxiety to distinguish Scottish policies from those in England:

I actually spoke recently at an event in Rome. It was the Italian group ... . And the subject was very much self-evaluation and I gave a presentation and talked about the Scottish context ... . And our English counterpart gave a presentation and talked about the PANDA system. And this incredible sort of complex ... machine and they were able to tell by the age of 11½ how youngsters will perform when they are x, y and z. (Interview with Scottish policy maker, September 2008)

Finally, apart from the informal contacts and exchanges, there was evidence of more formalized, contractual 'consultancy' work, through which Scotland has been spreading the 'self-evaluation' word around in Europe:

That was much more people, individual countries within that group being aware that Scotland was doing something they found quite interesting and productive and constructive. And they came to us and were interested. And therefore we've had this dialogue ... (Interview with Scottish policy maker, October 2008)

There is a lot of ... a lot of European links. And, for instance, and the visits to Scotland and the relationship will be of a number of different kinds. Some will be straightforward. A contract between us and, say, Malta and the Czech Republic to provide various services which involves staff development training. (Interview with Scottish policy maker, October 2008)

There is also referencing of the relationship between PISA and Scotland's influence in SICI from our interviewees:

Scotland is quite heavily engaged in SICI, it was involved in setting it up in the first place. It has grown as a forum for exchanging practice – particularly after the PISA shock – these countries looked at setting up national quality assurance bodies of some sort. There has tended to be quite a lot of exchange with inspectorates from other countries – Sweden came here, for example – Norwegians also looking at HGIOS. (Interview with Scottish policy maker, March 2009)

In explaining the popularity of the SSE model, one senior inspector identifies the persuasive power of the HGIOS text, and the fact that it is not an inspection guide:

I think the thing that attracted so much attention to the system here was just the way that HGIOS was produced as a very school focused, schools found it easy to use, accessible, written for schools system – an easy way of capturing data – and so HGIOS has been very much discussed and the momentum often translated – whereas other inspectorates – and you know in England – have tended to produce things that were written as inspection guidelines. (Interview with HMIE inspector, April 2009)

Discussion

At first sight the term 'self-evaluation' might give the impression of a 'bottom-up' approach to evaluation, and might be interpreted as providing evidence that teachers and school-management teams are reflective practitioners thinking about their own practice and shaping their practices on the basis of reflection on evidence. However, our interpretation of the Scottish system of self-evaluation using quality indicators set out in HGIOS is of an apparently permissive and negotiated system of evaluation that remains quite directive in its essential elements. Indeed, some critical commentators see it as a 'top-down system' using prescribed indicators rather than self-chosen goals (Cowie et al, 2007). The system could be described as producing not only knowledge about attainment but, importantly, knowledge about behaviours and attitudes – that is, 'a technology, a culture and a mode of regulation ... that employs judgements, comparisons, displays as means of control, attrition and change. The performances – of individual subjects or organisations – serve as measures of productivity or output, or displays of "quality"' (Ball, 2001, p 143). Further, a very significant aspect of self-evaluation is its travelling nature as well as its future orientation – it points towards movement, change and constant improvement that all schools and local authorities, across contexts and despite performance, need to plan and implement. In this sense, the HGIOS system of quality indicators often appears as encouraging schools to construct 'fabrications' of their performance which, either truly reflecting realities or not, they nevertheless fit into a very specific knowledge production regime which puts emphasis on constant self-regulation and self-improvement.

A number of points can be made about SSE as a travelling policy in Europe. Firstly, it is a resource for policy makers in relation to their ability to point to distinctive local (Scottish) practices and differences, as against more 'global' approaches, such as the indicators and benchmarking tools that come from the European Commission or the OECD. Of course, this is not to deny the importance of the self-evaluation model as a reflection of a distinctive ethos and idea of self-evaluation – this is without doubt the view of the Inspectorate, and one that they promote within and beyond Scotland. At the same time, it is interesting to note that attempts to steer the system through self-evaluation have been hindered in some contexts by the heavy hand of managerialism; in other cases and European contexts, we also observe a historic expectation of strong central influence that undercuts the discourse of a 'bottom-up' approach. This, in turn, creates a governance problem – the governance 'turn' is not unproblematic and is inserted into existing relations of ruling (Kooiman, 1993, Kohler-Koch & Eising, 1999). Thus, the harnessing of energies and commitment of the profession is inhibited by the perceived gap between policy rhetoric and its delivery and effects on professional practice. It will be interesting to explore the ways in which this dilemma is addressed.

Within the European education policy space, as in the wider arena and the emergent global education policy field, there is considerable sharing of ideas and approaches (Taylor et al, 1997; Alexiadiou & Jones 2001; Ozga & Lingard, 2007). A policy such as self-evaluation, developed in a small nation such as Scotland, can project a vision of the nation as distinctive and sophisticated abroad, that has benefits at home. In addition, the existence of key networks of expert policy brokers, such as SICI, enables the distribution of this approach far beyond the place of its original inception.

Finally, there are important points to be made about knowledge, and how it is mobilized in this new paradigm. As indicated above, we interpret this policy 'move' as a way for European inspectorates to recover lost ground and status: through the installation of self-evaluation they become the 'teachers' of the system. As one of them comments:

> We are in a unique position seeing so much front line practice across the whole country on a regular basis – we should capitalise on that evidence base by capturing the best and putting it back to others ... who can choose to adapt or follow it up or whatever. That spreading of best practice – in a way you can see HGIOS as an example of that – it's just us noting what we see as best practice in school improvement and turning it into a guidance toolkit and giving it back to people. (Interview with ex-HMIE inspector, May 2011)

They guide and support learning across institutions and authorities, and they return to a focus on process, which allows for much more latitude in terms of interpretation and translation. Exclusive reliance on data – which characterized the previous policy approach – limited the opportunities for European inspectorates to do anything other than pass judgement: their role was a monitoring and reporting one. With self-evaluation they move into developmental mode, with an orientation to a common European future, and the capacity to interpret the system to government. Governments themselves are committed to learning through evaluation of their progress against strategic directions, and inspectorates can bridge the gap between the emergent knowledge flowing from schools and authorities, and the political choices and actions that governments are impelled to take. This is a powerful, but high risk positioning. However, it is embraced by European inspectors, as this quotation from a senior inspector makes clear:

> But there's also a strong function, from my point of view, in
> informing policy development, managing policy development.
> For that reason, partly, we think it's good to have strong links
> with the department, ministers, as we currently do ... but
> always safeguarding to avoid political interference in what we
> say, which I think is quite necessary. (Interview with ex-HMIE
> inspector, May 2011)

SSE is used as a means of encoding school knowledge, creating 'compatibilities' – in this case a shared 'project' of self-improvement across Europe – and promoting self-managed and self-sufficient individuals (both teachers and pupils) in a decentralized, inclusive system. In other words, schools and their teachers and pupils become members of learning organizations, embedded within the larger learning organization of the local authority, of government and of Europe itself. The coding of knowledge through self-evaluation enables flows of knowledge within and across new European networks of knowledge production, like SICI. Furthermore, as schools and learners do more, they produce more and more new knowledge about themselves, which becomes productive for the constant improvement not only of the individual school, but for the governing of Europe as a whole.

The shift from centralized and vertical hierarchical forms of regulation to decentralized, horizontal, networked forms, noted in the literature on governance, also applies to knowledge. Yet, rather than representing the potential for democratization of either knowledge or governance, these forms closely resemble the networking practices, open communications and systems of global business, along with their increasing tendency to blur public and private distinctions. New data technologies and the promotion of learning organizations reflect the processes and instruments of knowledgeable/knowing capitalism and their 'economic imaginaries' and seek to establish new organizational forms that have 'a performative, constitutive force' (Jessop, 2008, p. 18).

Although data are crucial to the new governance, and reconstitute knowledge in governing form, the 'data dream' of infinite interoperability is disrupted by incompatibilities, by the inert mass of accumulated information and by the continued need for processes of brokering and translation of knowledge into action. The development and fast travel of self-evaluation in Europe may be understood as an attempt to address these problems, as well as the immediate financial crisis, by enrolling communities of practice in processes of constructing compatibilities through an emphasis on learning and self-evaluation, Further, the rise of knowledge-based professions and the brokering of knowledge by knowledge managers – in this case, European inspectorates – are both central in the development of knowledge-based governance in Europe.

CHAPTER 10

Conclusions

An argument about the wide-ranging and increasingly complex processes of the Europeanization of education has to start somewhere, and we chose to begin with its antecedents. The policies of the European Union, the work of the European Commission and the capacity and networking of its experts across Europe did not spring into action fully formed. European education policy grew out of national practices and understandings, and the work of academics and other professionals, as well as significant changes in circumstance and innovations.

Janne's idea of a 'normal space' was not just a political goal but a reflection of its time. Increasingly, European experts, as individuals or key members of national centres, had begun to collaborate in the post-war period, encouraged by political ideals and opportunities in a reconstructing Europe. The new 'normal space' to be constructed and in which to operate was a Europe of partnership and unities. They formed new European institutions, often closely associated with the USA, and reflecting its ideas and practices. Comparative research, surveys and academic leadership began to shape knowledge and expertise about European education. UNESCO, the IEA and the IIEP were all formed in the first post-war decade and the foundation of European education policy began in step with these rapidly consolidating institutions. When an education policy began to creep into existence, then those responsible could rely on the research work which preceded it – in cross-border comparative research, and the reconceptualization of education, including the new field of lifelong learning – and the continuing networks and associations of researchers.

Education, although at the margin of the European Community's broader policy agenda, was paving the way for integration through cooperation at a policy level, mobilizing networks, associations and a number of education players across Europe. Overcoming what Fragnière called the chaotic uniformity of European education, by creating an information service, and a European research infrastructure and policy, was the problem of the late 1980s and mid 1990s.

The idea of cooperation as a governing approach, distinctively educational, was built out of the impossibility of centralizing education policy and enforcing top-down decision making. The idea of a common cultural heritage and the unifying myths of the new imagined community were an important element in the drive to a broad brush education policy which did not threaten national autonomies.

At the same time, networks could both mobilize new actors, and if stable and successful, push Europeanizing processes wider and faster across different European scales and sites. If networks could remain pertinent and stable then new actors and significant platforms would be generated. The networks, their work, communications and platform, constituted a hub or 'home'. A home is a complex idea, involving social, cultural and work elements, associated with family and community, and most of all, with identity. The new European educators and researchers began to have homes which were not local, bounded or merely regional and national, they were also of a new European form.

Networks, projects and associations were important in producing the policy space of education. This was not a simple task as uncertainty and instability, created by new scale and organizational stresses, made effective entry and fresh opportunity hard to manage. Effective entry came at a cost. Cooperation and funding changed priorities, and constant engagement altered original purposes. The EU actively constructs European spaces which it is capable of governing at a distance. This is a disciplining effect, built on a soft and persuasive approach to governing. Fresh sites of European governance are built out of the thick web of networks and projects, and the products of data, standards and platforms. Building on agreed standards helps to create and extend the policy spaces which are being produced and governed across private and public arenas in new ways. The warp and weft of the European policy space in education is provided by the work of these experts, policy actors and ideas brokers, their instruments and their products.

The EU, through different parts of the European Commission, having provided a clear education policy in lifelong learning, has strengthened the education policy space by working with powerful partners, like the OECD, and reforming its own agencies, Eurostat and Eurydice. The rise of calculating and standardizing devices, following on from the open method of coordination, has extended the scale and reach of its political work, the management of the present and the calculation of the future. The new technology of the governance of the European education space through indicators and benchmarks has to be viewed as a deeply serious business of constructing new categories of (educational) thought and action – the project of reinventing a 'new' European identity of competitive advantage and responsible individualism. The birth of the EU's own education data production centre, the Joint Research Centre, combined with the growing effects of PISA across the governing of education in Europe's states, has produced constant comparison for improvement without the need for new or explicit forms of regulation in education. Indeed, the EU is not the only actor here. Professional groups now speed travelling policies around their communities, trying to solve local issues, but then enhancing the Europeanizing process. The shift from centralized and vertical hierarchical forms of regulation to decentralized, horizontal, networked forms also applies to knowledge. New data technologies and the promotion of learning organizations seek to provide material and performative force across education. Data and self-evaluation are the new political technologies, as is standardization, all part of a policy space in education now in Europe, built on governing knowledge and a new hidden politics of calculation.

The European space of education is now driven by the political work of producing the present and calculating the future. It is aiming to strengthen the national and value diversity, and it does not seek harmonization or a globalized uniformity. It is built on the same soft governing approach – it cajoles, persuades and enables – but it is powered by data and standards. Self-interest on the part of national governments, tempered by the need to avoid embarrassment and fit the local, has narrowed the gap between the European Commission and the Ministers of Education, in the search for economic competitiveness and a knowledge economy. Advances in the use of technologies for governing have reduced the secrecy and opacity of the local, and increased the transparency across the European policy space of education.

The networked busy web of communicative and associational space in European education, engaging professional and expert communities, has emerged over time. It now has a superstructure of institutions and agreements, a funding process and clear governing processes. It is still attracting engagement and it is still producing a governed policy space; persuasion and control are its mainstays but the politics of European education is often hidden by the instruments it uses. For many academics, teachers and researchers, European education does represent a homeland now, which their site of engagement may not any longer. Experts work with a portable expertise and they act as points of distribution for the ideas of Europeanization, creating, imagining, transmitting and producing. The space of flows has crystallized in the web and produced material effects in education.

Forms of European governance are difficult to disentangle or discover, and this is especially the case with the governance of education. Our argument is that at the moment when 'education' has ceased to be invisible as a governed object in European policy, it has been transformed in its scope and governance. The gradual shift from an indiscernible series of activities in the field of culture and education to a regulated space of learning via benchmarks and indicators is also a narrative about a shift in governance in Europe.

Globalization is a disruptive force for states, pushing aside progress and increasing uncertainties. The EU has acted as a new form of state, a transnational one, as a symbolic unity of all its constituents, but it has not been able to sustain a new encompassing idea that creates meaning for citizens. This is the force of Laïdi's argument about a 'world without meaning', the loss of a better future, of a symbolic way of representing it, and a future project. Yet it is possible that a space may be opened up that can be occupied by actors who find opportunities to create new meanings. Spaces of meaning have been created which are also symbolic spaces, transcending national spaces and striving to produce 'regional imaginaries'. Not enough is known yet about how this works in education, although there is evidence from professional and research groups, as we have shown.

This European education space is not an overall description of a known topography, containing fixed and identified elements, but instead, it describes a place coming into being, which has been catalysed into creation through a mode of ordering (Law, 1994).

This process may be seen culturally within Europe, as an exchange of ideas, as a desirable state, as a place in which the new European imaginary is mutually constructed and governance can be observed as a socially structured practice with material form. The focus on the political, administrative and economic form of the new Europe has often obscured this kind of cultural analysis, which emphasizes the processes of production and consumption of policy. Indeed, this book has explored European education as a project, not a condition or a situation; the exchange and construction of cultural narratives, across a range of areas, produces an imagined space, with a future-focused discourse, incorporating national symbols and calculated forms.

Notes

[1] Centre of Educational Research and Innovation (CERI). In Paris, in 1968, and then from 1971 within the OECD, CERI was a European based institution focused on the development of research activities in education and research/policy cooperation between Member countries. CERI initially worked mainly with professors of education in Europe, especially on pilot experiments in education and new conceptualizations in school innovation.

[2] Association des Enseignants et Chercheurs en Sciences de l'Education (AECSE) (the French Educational Research Association) was founded in 1971. The British Educational Research Association (BERA) was founded in 1974. Deutsche Gesellschaft für Erziehungswissenschaft (DGfE) (German Educational Research Association) was founded in 1963. The Nordic Educational Research Association (NERA) (Denmark, Finland, Iceland, Norway and Sweden), was founded in 1972. The Netherlands Educational Research Association (NERA) (Vereniging voor Onderwijs Research was founded in 1975.

[3] A European Commission resolution emphasized the significance of information sharing between Member States and the need for education statistics (OJ C 38, 19.2.1976). Eurostat started publishing data from national statistics in 1978; nonetheless, it was only after the 1990s that it began producing more statistically comparable data.

[4] This is the International Association for the Evaluation of Educational Achievement. Since its inception in 1958, the IEA has conducted more than 23 research studies of cross-national achievement. Examples are the Trends in Mathematics and Science Study (TIMMS, 1995, 1999, 2003, 2007) and the Progress in International Reading Literacy Studies (PIRLS, 2001, 2006).

[5] PIRLS was conducted in 2001 and 2006 by the IEA and aimed to measure the performance levels of pupils in reading comprehension in the fourth year of primary education.

[6] Eurostat website:
http://epp.eurostat.ec.europa.eu/portal/page/portal/about_eurostat/corpor ate/introduction/harmonization

[7] Eurydice website:
http://eacea.ec.europa.eu/education/eurydice/index_en.php

[8] Ibid.

[9] Ibid.

[10] http://ec.europa.eu/education/lifelong-learning-policy/doc32_en.htm

References

Adonnino, P. (1985) A People's Europe: Reports from the Ad Hoc Committee, Bulletin of the European Communities, Supplement 7/85. Luxembourg: Office for Official Publications of the European Communities.

Ahonen, P. (2001) Soft Governance, Agile Union? Analysis of the Extensions of Open Coordination in 2000. EIPA (European Institute of Public Administration), Maastricht, 18 April. http://unpan1.un.org/intradoc/groups/public/documents/nispacee/unpan007710.pdf

Alexiadou, N. & Jones, K. (2001) Travelling Policy/Local Spaces. Paper presented to the Congress Marx International 111, Le capitale et l'humanité, University of Paris X, September 26-29.

Ayral, M. (2005) International Cooperation in Standardisation – an indispensable tool in the global economy. Speech by Mr Michel Ayral, Director for Regulatory Policy at the European Commission, World Standards Day, Brussels, 14 October. http://ec.europa.eu/enterprise/policies/european-standards/files/international/world_standards_day/conferences/doc/2005/m_ayral_introduction_en.pdf

Ball, S.J. (1998) Big Policies/Small World: an introduction to international perspectives in education policy, *Comparative Education*, 34(2), 119-130.

Ball, S.J. (2001) Performativities and Fabrications in the Education Economy, in D. Gleeson & C. Husbands (Eds) *The Performing School: managing teaching and learning in a performance culture*, pp. 210-226. London: RoutledgeFalmer.

Barnett, M.N. & Finnemore, M. (1999) The Politics, Power and Pathologies of International Organisations, *International Organization*, 53(4), 699-732.

Bauman, Z. (1992) *Intimations of Postmodernity*. London: Routledge.

Bellier, I. & Wilson, T.W. (2000) *An Anthropology of the European Union: building, imagining and experiencing the New Europe*. Oxford: Berg.

Beukel, Erik (2001) Educational Policy: institutionalization and multi level governance, in Svein Andersen & Kjell Elliassen (Eds) *Making Policy in Europe*, 2nd edn. London: Sage.

Borzel, Tanja (1997) What's So Special about Policy Networks? An Exploration of the Concept and Its Usefulness in Studying European Governance, *European Integration online Papers* (EIoP), 1(16). http://eiop.or.at/eiop/pdf/1997-016.pdf

Brown, P., Halsey, A.H., Lauder, H. & Stuart Wells, A. (1997) The Transformation of Education and Society: an introduction, in A. Halsey, H. Lauder, P. Brown & A. Stuart Wells (Eds) *Education: culture, economy and society*. Oxford: Oxford University Press.

Brunsson, N. & Jacobsson, B. (Eds) (2000) *A World of Standards*. Oxford: Oxford University Press.

Burke, C. & Grosvenor, I. (2007) Designed Spaces and Disciplined Bodies: E.R. Robson's grand architectural tour, in: G. Timmerman, N. Bakker & J.J.H. Dekker (Ed.) *Cultuuroverdracht als pedagogisch motief. Historische en actuele perspectieven op onderwijs, sekse en beroep*. Groningen: Barkhuis.

Busch, L. (2007) Measuring Up: how standards shape our lives. Invited paper presented at the Economic and Social Research Council Genomics and Policy Forum, University of Edinburgh, May.

Byrne, D. & Ozga, J. (2008) Research and Policy: the BERA Academic Review 2006, *Research Papers in Education*, 23(4), 1-29.

Casey, C. (1995) *Work, Self and Society: after industrialism*. London and New York: Routledge.

Castells, M. (1996) *The Rise of the Network Society*. Oxford: Blackwell.

Centre Director's Annual Report, 2008/9 – Learning and Life Chances in Knowledge Economies and Societies (LLAKES), Economic and Social Research Council, 2009. http://www.esrc.ac.uk/my-esrc/grants/RES-594-28-0001/read/reports

Coombs, P. (1966) The International Institute for Educational Planning, *International Review of Education,* 12(3), 333-345. http://dx.doi.org/10.1007/BF01421541

Coombs, P. (1970) *What is Educational Planning?* Fundamentals of Educational Planning 1. Paris: International Institute for Educational Planning, UNESCO.

Corbett, A. (2005) *Universities and the Europe of Knowledge*. New York: Palgrave Macmillan.

Cort, P. (2010) Stating the Obvious: the European Qualifications Framework is *not* a neutral evidence-based policy tool, *European Educational Research Journal*, 9(3), 304-316. http://dx.doi.org/10.2304/eerj.2010.9.3.304

Council of the European Communities (1987) General Secretariat European Education Policy Statements, 3rd edn, June. Resolution of the Ministers of Education, November 1971, p. 11

Council of the European Union (2000a) Into the New Millennium': developing new working procedures for European cooperation in the field of education and training, *Official Journal of the Communities*, 8, 12 January.

Council of the European Union (2000b) Lisbon European Council, 23 and 24 March 2000. Presidency Conclusions. http://www.europarl.europa.eu/summits/lis1_en.htm

Council of the European Union (2001) The Concrete Future Objectives of Education and Training Systems. Report from the Education Council to the European Council, 14 February, 5980/01, EDUC 23. http://ec.europa.eu/education/policies/2010/doc/rep_fut_obj_en.pdf

Council of the European Union (2004) 'Education and Training 2010': the success of the Lisbon strategy hinges on urgent reforms. Joint interim report of the Council and the Commission on the implementation of the detailed work programme on the follow up of the objectives of education and training systems in Europe, Brussels, 3 March, 6905/04, EDUC 43.
http://ec.europa.eu/education/policies/2010/doc/jir_council_final.pdf

Council of the European Union (2006) Presidency Conclusions. Brussels 10633/1/06 REV 1.
http://www.consilium.europa.eu/ueDocs/cms_Data/docs/pressData/en/ec/90 111.pdf

Council of the European Union (2008) Presidency Conclusions. Brussels 14368/08.
http://www.consilium.europa.eu/uedocs/cms_data/docs/pressdata/en/ec/10 3441.pdf

Council of the European Union (2009) Council Conclusions of 12 May 2009 on a Strategic Framework for European Cooperation in Education and Training ('ET 2020') (2009/C 119/02), Official Journal of the European Union, C 119/2.

Cowie, M. (2001) Talking Heads: a critical analysis of the quality assurance relationship between headteachers and an education authority. Research Paper 5. Aberdeen: Centre for Educational Research, University of Aberdeen.

Cowie, M., Taylor, D. & Croxford, L. (2007) 'Tough, Intelligent Accountability' in Scottish Secondary Schools and the Role of Standard Tables and Charts (STACS): a critical appraisal, *Scottish Educational Review*, 39(1), 29-50.

Cram, L. (1998) The EU Institutions and Collective Action; constructing a European interest? in J. Greenwood, & M. Aspinwall (Eds) *Collective Action in the European Union*, 63-80. London: Routledge.

Croxford, L., Grek, S. & Shaik, F.J. (2009) Quality Assurance and Evaluation (QAE) in Scotland: promoting self-evaluation within and beyond the country, *Journal of Education Policy*, 24(2), 179-193.

Dahler-Larsen, P. (2005) Evaluation and Public Management, in: E. Ferlie, L. Lynn & C. Pollitt (Eds) *The Oxford Handbook of Public Management*, 615-642. Oxford: Oxford University Press.

Dale, R. (2006) Policy Relationships between Supranational and National Scales; Imposition/Resistance or Parallel Universes?, in J. Kallo & R. Rinne (Eds) *Supranational Regimes and National Education Policies: encountering challenge*. Research in Educational Sciences 24, pp. 27-52. Helsinki: Finnish Educational Research Association.

Dale, R. (2009) Contexts, Constraints, and Resources in the Development of European Education Space and European Education Policy, in R. Dale & S. Robertson (Eds) *Globalisation and Europeanisation in Education*. Oxford: Symposium Books.

Davies, H. (2004) Is Evidence-Based Government Possible? Jerry Lee lecture, 4th Annual Campbell Collaboration Colloquium, Washington, DC.

Davies, H., Nutley, S. & Smith, P. (2000) *What Works? Evidence-Based Policy and Practice in Public Services*. Bristol: Policy Press.

Delanty, G. (1995) *Inventing Europe: idea, identity, reality*. London: Macmillan.

Delanty, G. & Rumford, C. (2005) *Rethinking Europe: social theory and the implications of Europeanization*. London: Routledge.

Desrosières, A. (1998) *The Politics of Large Numbers: a history of statistical reasoning*. Cambridge, MA: Harvard University Press.

Eising, R. & Kohler-Koch, B. (1999) Network Governance in the European Union, in B. Kohler-Koch & R. Eising (Eds) *The Transformation of Governance in the European Union*, pp. 3-13. London: Routledge.

European Commission (1979) *The European Community and Education*. European File. Luxembourg: Office for Official Publications of the European Communities.

European Commission (1982) *An Education Policy for Europe*. European Documentation Series. Luxembourg: Office for Official Publications of the European Communities.

European Commission (1996) Towards the Learning Society. White Paper on Education and Training, Teaching and Learning. European Commission DGXXII. http://www.cec.lu/en/comm/dg22/lbhp.htm

European Commission (1997) Towards a Europe of Knowledge. Communication from the Commission. COM(97)563.

European Commission (2001a) Towards a Europe of Knowledge. Report of the Eurostat Taskforce on Measuring Lifelong Learning. COM(97)563 Part 2.

European Commission (2001b) Towards a European Research Area - Key Figures 2001 - Special edition: Indicators for benchmarking of national research policies. Luxembourg: Office for Publications of the European Communities. http://ec.europa.eu/research/era/pdf/benchmarking2001.pdf

European Commission (2001c) European Governance. A White Paper. COM(2001) 428. http://ec.europa.eu/governance/white_paper/en.pdf

European Commission (2001d) *European Report on Quality of School Education – 16 quality indicators*. Report based on the work of the Working Committee on Quality Indicators, May 2000. Luxembourg: Office for Official Publications of the European Communities.

European Commission (2001e) Making a European Area of Lifelong Learning a Reality. COM(2001) 678 final

European Commission (2002a) *Education and Training in Europe: diverse systems, shared goals for 2010. The Work Programme on the Future Objectives of Education and Training Systems*. Luxembourg: Office for Official Publications of the European Communities.

European Commission (2002b) *The Future Development of the European Union Education, Training and Youth Programmes after 2006 – a public consultation document*. Luxembourg: Office for Official Publications of the European Communities.

European Commission (2002c) European Benchmarks in Education and Training. Follow-up to the Lisbon European Council. Communication from the Commission. COM (2002) 629 final. Luxembourg: Office for Official Publications of the European Communities.

European Commission (2003) Education and Training 2010. Staff working paper, SEC2003 1250. Luxembourg: Office for Official Publications of the European Communities.

European Commission (2004a) Delivering Lisbon – reforms for the enlarged Union. Report from the Commission to the spring European Council, COM(2004) 29 Final/2, 20 February.

European Commission (2004b) Progress towards the Common Objectives in Education and Training: indicators and benchmarks. Staff working paper. SEC (2004) 73.

European Commission (2005a) Working Together for Growth and Jobs: integrated guidelines for growth and jobs (2005-8). Communication to the spring European Council. http://europa.eu.int/growthandjobs/ (accessed 28 November 2006).

European Commission (2005b) Progress towards the Lisbon Objectives in Education and Training. Staff working paper. SEC (2005) 419.

European Commission (2005c) Lisbon National Reform Programmes for Growth and Jobs 2005-08. http://www.central2013.eu/fileadmin/user_upload/Downloads/Tools_Resou rces/Lisbon_MEMO-06-23_EN_1_.pdf

European Commission (2005d) Task Force Report on Adult Education Survey. Luxembourg. http://epp.eurostat.ec.europa.eu/cache/ITY_OFFPUB/KS-CC-05-005/EN/KS-CC-05-005-EN.PDF

European Commission (2006a) *The History of European Cooperation in Education and Training. Europe in the Making: an example.* Luxembourg: Office for Official Publications of the European Communities.

European Commission (2006b) Time to Move up a Gear: the new partnership for growth and jobs. Communication from the Commission to the spring European Council. Luxembourg: Office for Official Publications of the European Communities.

European Commission (2008) Key Activity 1 Transversal Programme 2008 – Studies and Comparative Research; Award of grants for actions to develop and implement the European Qualifications Framework (EQF); National Lifelong Learning Strategies (NLLS). http://eacea.ec.europa.eu/llp/funding/2008/call/index_en.htm

European Commission/Eurostat (2001) Report of the Eurostat Taskforce on Measuring Lifelong Learning. http://www.clab.edc.uoc.gr/hy302/papers/lifelong%20learning%20in%20E U%20report%202001.pdf

European Commission-SICI (2001) School Self-Evaluation in Thirteen Countries/Regions. Brussels: Directorate-General for Education and Culture

European Council (1983) Solemn Declaration on European Union. Stuttgart, 19 June 1983. Bulletin of the European Communities, No. 6/1983. pp. 24-29.

European Council (1984a) Television without Frontiers. Green Paper on the Establishment of the Common Market for Broadcasting. Part Six. COM (84) 300 final/Part 5, 14 June 1984.

European Council (1984b) Conclusions of the Fontainebleau European Council (25 and 26 June 1984). Bulletin of the European Communities, June 1984, no. 6. Luxembourg: Office for Official Publications of the European Communities.

European Council (2004) 'Education & Training 2010'. The Success of the Lisbon Strategy Hinges on Urgent Reforms. Joint interim report of the Council and the Commission, 14358/03 EDUC 168 – COM (2003) 685 final.

European Education Projects [EEPs] (1987) Comenius Action 1.

European Network of Policy Makers for the Evaluation of Education Systems (2004) Reporting Evaluation Findings to Policy Makers. Network study. http://cisad.adc.education.fr/reva/english/index.htm (accessed 10 February 2007).

European Schoolnet (2002a) *Re-engineering Learning in Schools and Society.* Networking event in IST 2002 (European Commission Information Society Technologies Programme).

European Schoolnet (2002b) *The THINK Report: Technology in Education Futures for Policy.* Professor David Wood. http://resources.eun.org/insight/think_report.pdf

European Schoolnet (2006) Roadmap to Interoperability to Education in Europe. http://www.intermedia.uio.no/download/attachments/8401/LIFE_BOOK_on_web.pdf

Eurydice/Eurostat/European Commission (2000) Key Data on Education in Europe. Luxembourg: Office for Official Publications of the European Communities.

Eurydice/Eurostat/European Commission (2002) Key Data on Education in Europe. Luxembourg: Office for Official Publications of the European Communities.

Eurydice/Eurostat/European Commission (2005) Key Data on Education in Europe. Luxembourg: Office for Official Publications of the European Communities.

Fairclough, N. (2000) *New Labour, New Language?* London: Routledge.

Federal Ministry of Education and Research. http://www.bmbf.de/en/3292.php

Finnemore, M. (1993) International Organisations as Teachers of Norms: UNESCO and science policy, *International Organization*, 47(4), 565-597.

Finnish Ministry of Education. http://www.minedu.fi/OPM/ (accessed 25 January 2007).

Fogg, K. & Jones, H. (1985) Ten Years On: changing issues in education, 1975-1985, *European Journal of Education*, 20(2/3), European Institute of Education and Social Policy Tenth Anniversary Issue, 293-300.

Forrest, Alan (1993) New Role for Education in the European Community. Lecture to the Cumbrian Branch of the Cambridge Society in Brussels, cited in L. Pépin (2006) *The History of European Cooperation in Education and Training: Europe in the making – an example*, p. 16. Luxembourg: Office for Official Publications of the European Communities.

Foucault, M., Martin, L.H., Gutman, H. & Hutton, P.H. (1988) *Technologies of the Self: a seminar with Michel Foucault*. Amhurst, MA: University of Massachusetts Press.

Fragnière, G. (1979) Is it Too Early for a European Education Policy? Editorial, *European Journal of Education*, 14(4), 311-312.

Grek, S. (2009) Governing by Numbers: the PISA effect in Europe, *Journal of Education Policy*, 24(1), 23-37.

Grek, S. (2010) International Organisations and the Shared Construction of Policy 'Problems': problematisation and change in education governance in Europe, *European Educational Research Journal*, 9(3), 396-406.

Grek, S., Ozga, J. & Lawn, M. (2009a) Integrated Children's Services in Scotland. KnowandPol Orientation 2, Public Action 1. http://www.knowandpol.eu/fileadmin/KaP/content/Scientific_reports/Orientation2/O2.PA1.Scotland_educ.FV.English_version.pdf (Accessed 9 June 2010).

Grek, S., Lawn, M., Lingard, B., Ozga, J., Rinne, R., Segerholm, C. & Simola, H. (2009b) National Policy Brokering and the Construction of the European Education Space in England, Sweden, Finland and Scotland, *Comparative Education*, 45(1), 5-21.

Gretler, A. (1999a) Some Information on the EERA-Inquiry into 'Structure and Organisation of Educational R&D in European Countries'. Paper presented at European Conference on Educational Research, 22-25 September, in Lahti.

Gretler, A. (1994b) Minutes of the Second Meeting of Representatives of National Educational Research Associations in European Countries (14-15 October in Aarau, Switzerland).

Gretler, Armin (2007) The International Social Organization of Educational Research in Europe: reviewing the European Educational Research Association as an example – facts and questions, *European Educational Research Journal*, 6(2), 174-189.

Group of Political Analysis (GPA) (2012) http://ec.europa.eu/dgs/policy_advisers/experts_groups/gpa_en.htm

Gwyn, R. (1979) Towards a European Policy for Initial Teacher Education: scope and constraints, *European Journal of Education*, 14(4), 359-368.

Hacking, I. (1975) *The Emergence of Probability*. Cambridge: Cambridge University Press.

Hacking, I. (1990) *The Taming of Chance*. Cambridge: Cambridge University Press.

Hacking, I. (1991) How Should We Do the History of Statistics? in G. Burchell, C. Gordon & P. Miller (Eds) *The Foucault Effect: studies in governmentality*. London: Harvester Wheatsheaf.

Henry, M., Lingard, B., Taylor, S. & Rizvi, F. (2001) *The OECD, Globalisation and Education* Policy. Oxford: Pergamon.

Higgins, V. & Larner, W. (Eds) (2010) *Calculating the Social: standards and the reconfiguration of governing*. Basingstoke: Palgrave Macmillan.

Hingel, Anders (2001) *Education Policies and European Governance*. Brussels: European Commission – Directorate-General for Education and Culture.

Husén, T. (1983) International Context of Educational Research, *Oxford Review of Education*, 9(1), 21-29.

Janne, H. (1973) For a Community Policy on Education. Bulletin of the European Communities Supplement 10/73. http://aei.pitt.edu/5588/1/5588.pdf

Jensen, O. & Richardson, T. (2004) *Making European Space: mobility, power and territorial identity*. London: Routledge.

Jessop, Bob (2008) The Knowledge-Based Economy, *Naked Punch*, 10. http://eprints.lancs.ac.uk/1007/1/Microsoft_Word_-_I-2008_Naked_Punch.pdf

Jessop, B., Brenner, N. & Jones, M. (2008) Theorizing Socio-Spatial Relations, *Environment and Planning D: Society and Space*, 26(3), 389-401.

Jones, P.D. (2010) The European Commission and Education Policy in the European Union: an ethnographic discourse analysis. PhD thesis, Bristol.

Jones, P.W. (2007) Education and World Order, *Comparative Education*, 43(3), 325-337.

Kandel, I. (1955) National and International Aspects of Education, *International Review of Education*, 1(1), 5-17.

Knill, C. (2001) *The Europeanisation of National Administrations: patterns of institutional change and persistence*. Cambridge: Cambridge University Press.

Kohler-Koch, B. & Eising, R. (Eds) (1999) *The Transformation of Governance in the European Union*. London: Routledge.

Kok, W. et al (2004) *Facing the Challenge: the Lisbon strategy for growth and employment. Report from the High Level Group chaired by Wim Kok*. http://ec.europa.eu/growthandjobs/pdf/kok_report_en.pdf (accessed 25 November 2006).

Kooiman, T. (Ed.) (1993) *Modern Governance: new government–society interactions*. London: Sage.

Laïdi, Z. (1998) *A World without Meaning: the crisis of meaning in international politics*. London: Routledge.

Laïdi, Z. (2003) The Delocalization of Meaning, in P. Mandaville & A. Williams (Eds) *Meaning and International Relations*. London and New York: Routledge.

Landsheere, G. de (n.d.) IEA & UNESCO: a history of working cooperation. http://www.unesco.org/education/pdf/LANDSHEE.PDF

Lascoumes, P. & Le Galès, P. (2007) Understanding Public Policy through its Instruments: from the nature of instruments to the sociology of public policy instrumentation, *Governance*, 20(1), 1-21. http://dx.doi.org/10.1111/j.1468-0491.2007.00342.x

Law, J. (1994) *Organizing Modernity*. Oxford: Blackwell.

Lawn, M. (2001a) Borderless Education: imagining a European education space in a time of brands and networks, *Discourse*, 22(2), 173-184.

Lawn, M. (2001b) Effective Networking: sustaining EERA as a network in the European Educational Research Space. ECER Lille, EERJ Roundtable.

Lawn, M. (2003) The 'Usefulness' of Learning: the struggle over governance, meaning and the European education space, *Discourse*, 24(3), 325-336. http://dx.doi.org/10.1080/0159630032000172515

Lawn, M. (2006) Soft Governance and the Learning Spaces of Europe, *Comparative European Politics*, 4(2-3), 272-288. http://dx.doi.org/10.1057/palgrave.cep.6110081

Lawn, M. (2007) Governing by Association in Europe? The Problems of the Unstable Policy Network, Critical Studies in Education, 1, 79-95. http://dx.doi.org/10.1080/17508480601120962

Lawn, M. (2008) An Intellectual Homeland: governing mobilities and space in European education, in C. Rumford (Ed.) *The Sage Handbook of European Studies*. London: Sage.

Lawn, M. & Lingard, B. (2002) Constructing a European Policy Space in Educational Governance: the role of transnational policy actors, *European Educational Research Journal*, 1(2), 290-307.

Leibrandt, G. (1982) European Co-operation in Higher Education: an assessment of future needs, *European Journal of Education*, 17(1), 23-26.

Leonard, M. (1998) *Europe: the search for European identity*. London: Demos.

Lingard, B. & Grek, S. (2007) The OECD, Indicators and PISA: an exploration of events and theoretical perspectives. Fabricating Quality in European Education, Working Paper 2. http://www.ces.ed.ac.uk/research/FabQ/publications.htm (accessed 29 September 2007).

Lingard, B. & Rawolle, S. (2004) Mediatizing Educational Policy: the journalistic field, science policy, and cross-field effects, *Journal of Education Policy*, 19(3), 361-380.

Lingard, B., Rawolle, S. & Taylor, S. (2005) Globalizing Policy Sociology in Education: working with Bourdieu, *Journal of Education Policy*, 20(6), 759-777.

Lloyd, W.A. (1964) The Exchange and Publication of Research Work in the Field of Education, *International Review of Education*, 10(2), 221-224.

Mamadouh, V. & Van der Wusten, H. (2008) The European Level in EU Governance: territory, authority and trans-scalar networks, *GeoJournal*, 72, 19-31.

Martens, K. (2007) How to Become an Influential Actor: the 'comparative turn' in OECD education policy, in K. Martens, A. Rusconi & K. Lutz (Eds) *Transformations of the State and Global Governance*, 40-56. London: Routledge.

Miller, P. & Rose, N. (2008) *Governing the Present: administering economic, social and personal life*. Cambridge: Polity Press.

Nairn, T. (1981) *The Break-up of Britain: crisis and neonationalism*. London: Verso.

Normand, Romuald (2010) Expertise, Networks and Indicators: the construction of the European strategy in education, *European Educational Research Journal*, 9(3), 407-421. http://dx.doi.org/10.2304/eerj.2010.9.3.407

Nóvoa, António (1996) The Construction of the European: changing patterns of identity through Europe, in H. Simola & T. Popkewitz (Eds) *Professionalisation and Education*, pp. 28-51. Helsinki: Department of Teacher Education, University of Helsinki.

Nóvoa, António (2000) The Restructuring of the European Educational Space, in Thomas Popkewitz (Ed.) *Educational Knowledge: changing relationships between the state, civil society, and the educational community*, pp. 31-57. New York: Suny Press.

Nóvoa, A. & Lawn, M. (Eds) (2002) *Fabricating Europe: the formation of an education space*. Dordrecht: Kluwer.

Nóvoa, A. & Yariv-Mashal, T. (2003) Comparative Research in Education: a mode of governance or a historical journey, *Comparative Education*, 39(4), 423-438.

Nutley, S., Davies, H. & Walter, I. (2002) Evidence-Based Policy and Practice: cross-sector lessons from the UK. Keynote paper for the Social Policy Research and Evaluation Conference, 2-3 July, in Wellington, New Zealand.

Nye, J. (2004) *Soft Power: the means to success in world politics*. New York: Public Affairs.

Organization for Economic Cooperation and Development (OECD) (1999) Classifying Educational Programmes Manual for ISCED-97 Implementation in OECD Countries, Paris: OECD. http://www.oecd.org/dataoecd/7/2/1962350.pdf

Organization for Economic Cooperation and Development (OECD) (2001) *Knowledge and Skills for Life: first results of Programme for International Student Assessment*. Paris: OECD.

Organization for Economic Cooperation and Development (OECD) (2003) *What is PISA?* http://www.pisa.oecd.org/dataoecd/51/27/37474503.pdf (accessed 15 October 2007).

Organization for Economic Cooperation and Development (OECD) (2000) *Knowledge Management in the Learning Society*. Paris: OECD.

Ozga, J. & Lingard, B. (2007) Globalisation, Education Policy and Politics, in B. Lingard & J. Ozga (Eds) *The RoutledgeFalmer Reader in Education Policy and Politics*. London: Routledge.

Ozga, J., Dahler-Larsen, P., Segerholm, C. & Simola, H. (Eds) (2011) *Fabricating Quality in Education: data and governance in Europe*. London: Routledge.

Pépin, L. (2006) *The History of European Cooperation in Education and Training: Europe in the making – an example*. Luxembourg: Office for Official Publications of the European Communities.

Petit, I. (2007) Mimicking History: the European Commission and its education policy, *World Political Science Review*, 3(1), 1-25.

Plomp, T. (1991) Educational Research in Europe: possibilities for facilitating exchange of information and researchers. Prepared for the Commission of the

European Communities Task Forces Human Resources, Education, Training and Youth, 11 October. Berlin: EERA archives.

Plomp, T. (1992) Conclusions of Meeting of Representatives of National and International Associations of Educational Researchers. University of Twente, Enschede, 22 June.

Pongratz, L. (2006) Voluntary Self-control: education reform as a governmental strategy, *Education Philosophy and Theory*, 38(4), 471-482.

Porter, T. (1995) *Trust in Numbers*. Princeton: Princeton University Press.

Porter, T. & Webb, M. (2004) The Role of the OECD in the Orchestration of Global Knowledge Networks. Paper prepared for the International Studies Association Annual Meeting, September, in Montreal.

Power, M. (2003a) Auditing and the Production of Legitimacy, *Accounting, Organizations and Society*, 28, 379-394.

Power, M. (2003b) Evaluating the Audit Explosion, *Law and Policy*, 25(3), 185-202.

Power, M. (2004) Counting, Control and Calculation: reflections on measuring and management, *Human Relations*, 57, 765-783.

Prenzel, M., Drechsel, B., Carstensen C.H. & Ramm, G. (2004) PISA 2003: Eine Einführung, in M. Prenzel, J. Baumert, W. Blum, et al (Eds) *PISA 2003. Der Bildungsstand der Jugendlichen in Deutschland: Ergebnisse des zweiten internationalen Vergleichs*. Münster:Waxmann.

Power, M. (1999) *The Audit Society: rituals of verification*. Oxford: Oxford University Press.

Reich, Robert B. (1991) *The Work of Nations*. New York: Alfred A. Knopf.

Rhodes, R. (1996) The New Governance: governing without government, *Political Studies*, 4(4), 652-667.

Rinne, R. (2007) The Growing Supranational Impacts of the OECD and the EU on National Educational Policies and a Case of Finland. Paper presented at the Nordic Educational Research Association conference, Turku University, 15-17 March.

Rinne, R., Kallo, J. & Hokka, S. (2004) Too Eager to Comply? OECD Education Policies and the Finnish Response, *European Educational Research Journal*, 3(2), 454-485.

Rizvi, F. & Lingard, B. (2006) Globalisation and the Changing Nature of the OECD's Educational Work, in H. Lauder, P. Brown, J. Dillabough & A.H. Halsey (Eds) *Education, Globalisation and Social Change*. Oxford: Oxford University Press.

Robertson, S.L. (2007) Embracing the Global: crisis and the creation of a new semiotic order to secure Europe's knowledge-based economy. Bristol: Centre for Globalisation, Education and Societies, University of Bristol. http://www.bris.ac.uk/education/people/academicStaff/edslr/publications/12slr/

Rosamond, B. (2003) End of Award Report to ESRC on Globalisation, EU Economic Policy Communities and the Construction of European Identities (award no. L213252024). http://www.esrc.ac.uk/

Rose, N. (1991) Governing by Numbers: figuring out society, *Accounting Organisation and Society*, 15(7), 673-692.

Rose, N. (1992) Governing the Enterprising Self, in P. Heelas & P. Morris (Eds) *The Values of the Enterprise Culture*. London: Routledge.

Sassen, S. (2007) *Deciphering the Global: its scales, spaces and subjects*. London: Routledge.

Schuller, T. & Burns, T. (Eds) (2007) *Evidence in Education: linking research and policy*. Paris: Organization for Economic Cooperation and Development.

Scimeca, S., Dumitru, P, Durando, M. et al (2009) European Schoolnet: enabling school networking, *European Journal of Education*, 44(4), 475-492.

Scottish Executive Education Department (2002) *PISA –Scottish* report. Edinburgh: Scottish Executive.

Scottish Office Education Department (SOED) (1991a) *The Role of School Development Plans in Managing School Effectiveness*. Edinburgh: HMSO, HM Inspectors of Schools.

Scottish Office Education Department (SOED) (1991b) *Using Examination Results in School Self-evaluation: relative ratings and national comparison factors*. Edinburgh: HMSO, HM Inspectors of Schools.

Scottish Office Education Department (SOED) (1994a) School Development Plans. Circular and Guidelines. Circular No 1/94. Edinburgh: HMSO.

Scottish Office Education Department (SOED) (1994b) The Role of School Development Plans in Managing School Effectiveness, 2nd edn. Edinburgh: HMSO, HM Inspectors of Schools.

Scottish Office Education and Industry Department (SOEID) (1996) *How Good is Our School? Self-evaluation Using Performance Indicators*. Edinburgh: Audit Unit, HMSO, HM Inspectors of Schools.

Scottish Office Education and Industry Department (SOEID) (1997) The Quality Initiative in Scottish Schools (QISS). Final draft of a QISS discussion paper presented at a seminar organised by HM Inspectors of Schools, Audit Unit, 10 June, in Edinburgh.

Scottish Office Education and Industry Department (SOEID) (1999) *Closing the Circle: a report by HM Inspectors of Schools on the management of quality improvement by education authorities in Scotland*. Edinburgh: HMSO, HM Inspectors of Schools.

Scottish Parliament (2000) Standards in Scotland's Schools etc. Act. http://www.opsi.gov.uk/legislation/scotland/acts2000/20000006.htm (accessed 23 February 2009).

Segerholm, C. (2003) To Govern in Silence? An Essay on the Political in National Evaluations of the Public Schools in Sweden, *Studies in Educational Policy and Educational Philosophy E-tidskrift*, 2003:2. http://upi.ped.uu.se/SITE_Docs/Doc184.pdf

Shore, Cris (2000) *Building Europe: the cultural politics of European integration*. London: Routledge.

Simola, H. (2005) The Finnish Miracle of PISA: historical and sociological remarks on teaching and teacher education, *Comparative Education*, 41(4), 455–470.

Standing International Conference of Inspectorates (SICI) (2000) Newsletter. http://www.sici-inspectorates.org/ww/en/pub/sici/publication/newsletter_archive.htm (accessed 2 June 2010).

Standing International Conference of Inspectorates (SICI) (2003) The Effective School Self-Evaluation project. Brussels: European Commission.

Standing International Conference of Inspectorates (SICI) (2005) SICI Workshop on Effective School Self-Evaluation (ESSE). Report of the SICI Workshop held in Copenhagen, 20-21 January. http://www.sici-inspectorates.org/ww/en/pub/sici/publication/workshop_reports_since_2006.htm (accessed 2 June 2010).

Steiner-Khamsi, G. (2004) *The Global Politics of Educational Borrowing and Lending*. Columbia: Teachers College Press.

Stone, D. (2004) Transfer Agents and Global Networks in the 'Transnationalization' of Policy', *Journal of European Public Policy*, 11(3), 545-566.

Strathern, M. (2004) *Commons and Borderlands: working papers on interdisciplinarity, accountability and the flow of knowledge*. Wantage: Sean Kingston Publishing.

Strathern, M. (Ed.) (2000) *Audit Cultures: anthropological studies in accountability, ethics and the academy*. London: Routledge.

Taylor, S., Rizvi, F., Lingard, B. & Henry, M. (1997) *Education Policy and the Politics of Change*. London: Routledge.

Teachernet (2007) http://www.teachernet.gov.uk/ (accessed 28 January 2007).

Tersmette, E. (2001) Benchmarking of Quality of Education: a European perspective. International Meeting on the occasion of the 200th anniversary of the Netherlands Inspectorate of Education, Inspecting in a New Age, 19 October, in Utrecht.

Treaty of Amsterdam: Amending the Treaty on European Union, the Treaties establishing the European Communities and certain related acts. Amsterdam, 2 October 1997. http://www.eurotreaties.com/amsterdamtreaty.pdf

Tucker, C. (2003) The Lisbon Strategy and the Open Method of Coordination: a new vision and the revolutionary potential of soft governance in the European Union. Paper prepared for the 2003 Annual Meeting of the American Political Science Association, August 28-31, in Philadelphia.

Välijärvi, J. et al (2002) *The Finnish Success in PISA –and some reasons behind it*. Jyväskylä: Institute for Educational Research, University of Jyväskylä.

Walters, W. & Haahr, J.H. (2005) *Governing Europe. discourse, governmentality and European integration*. London: Routledge.

Weir, D. (2008) Her Majesty's Inspectorate of Education, in T. Bryce & W. Humes (Eds) *Scottish Education*, 3rd edn, pp. 142-151. Edinburgh: Edinburgh University Press.

Wuttke, J. (2006) Fehler, Verzerrungen, Unsicherheiten in der PISA Auswertung, in T. Jahnke & W. Meyerhöfer (Eds) *PISA & Co: Kritik eines Programms*, 101-154. Hildesheim: Franzbecker.

Ydesen, C. (2012) The International Space of the Danish Testing Community in the Interwar Years, *Paedagogica Historica*, 48(2).

Notes on the Authors

MARTIN LAWN is Professorial Research Fellow, Centre for Educational Sociology, University of Edinburgh and Senior Research Fellow, Department of Education, University of Oxford. After teaching at a London comprehensive school, he has since worked at the University of Edinburgh and the University of Birmingham, with Visiting Professorships in Sweden, Finland and Argentina. He is an ex-Secretary General of the European Educational Research Association (EERA). Martin is currently editor of the association's *European Educational Research Journal* (www.wwwords.eu/EERJ).

SOTIRIA GREK is a Lecturer in Social Policy at the School of Social and Political Science, University of Edinburgh. Her research interests lie in the areas of education governance; education and European integration; analysis of education policy discourses; museum education; and education and social change. Prior to her current position, Sotiria worked as a Research Fellow in Education Policy and Politics at the Centre for Educational Sociology (CES) at the University of Edinburgh.

Acknowledgement

Both authors would like to acknowledge the Economic and Social Research Council (ESRC) for supporting their research through the following project grants: 'Governing by Numbers: data and education governance in Scotland and England' (2006-2009) (RES-000-23-1385); 'Transnational Policy Learning: a comparative study of OECD and EU education policy in constructing the skills and competencies agenda' (2010-2012) (RES-000-22-3429); and 'Governing by Inspection: school inspection and education governance in Scotland, England and Sweden' (2010-2013) (RES-062-23-2241).